The ESSENTIALS® of

Financial Management

Omer L. Carey, Ph.D.
Chairperson of Management Science Department
Alaska Pacific University, Anchorage, Alaska

Musa M. H. Essayyad, Ph.D.
Associate Professor of Finance
University of Alaska, Anchorage, Alaska

Research & Education Association
61 Ethel Road West
Piscataway, New Jersey 08854

THE ESSENTIALS®
OF FINANCIAL MANAGEMENT

Year 2005 Printing

Printed in the United States of America

Library of Congress Control Number 00-133920

International Standard Book Number 0-87891-724-1

B05

What REA's Essentials®
Will Do for You

This book is part of REA's celebrated *Essentials*® series of review and study guides, relied on by tens of thousands of students over the years for being complete yet concise.

Here you'll find a cogent summary of the very material you're most likely to need for exams, not to mention homework—eliminating the need to read and review many pages of textbook and class notes.

This slim volume condenses the vast amount of detail characteristic of the subject matter and summarizes the **essentials** of the field. The book provides quick access to the important facts, terms, theorems, concepts, and formulas in the field.

It will save you hours of study and preparation time.

This *Essentials*® book has been prepared by experts in the field and has been carefully reviewed to ensure its accuracy and maximum usefulness. We believe you'll find it a valuable, handy addition to your library.

Larry B. Kling
Chief Editor

Acknowledgment

We would like to thank Robert Volk for his editorial contributions.

CONTENTS

iv

CHAPTER 1

THE FUNCTION AND GOALS OF FINANCIAL MANAGEMENT

1.1   THE FIELD OF FINANCE

Finance is the art and science of managing money. Finance applies the disciplines of economics and accounting to various problems in the firm.

There are two major areas in finance.

One of the areas is the provision of financial services to individuals, businesses, nonprofit organizations and government. The major opportunities in financial services are:

1. Banks, savings and loans, and similar institutions.

2. Personal financial planning. Certified Financial Planners are professionals in this activity.

3. Investments. Stockbrokers, financial analysts and portfolio managers are some of the jobs available in this area. The Chartered Financial Analyst is the professional designation in financial analysis and portfolio management.

4. Real estate and insurance, brokers, property managers, appraisers and planners are some of the job opportunities in real estate. There are several professional designations in real estate. Agents, brokers, underwriters and claims service are some of the job opportunities in insurance. Chartered Life Underwriter (CLU) and Chartered Property and Casualty Underwriter (CPCU) are the two major professional designations in insurance.

Financial management is the second of these two major areas. A fi-

1

nancial manager manages the financial affairs of any type of business, whether financial or nonfinancial, private or public, profit or nonprofit.

1.2 THE FINANCIAL MANAGER'S RESPONSIBILITIES

The main responsibilities of the financial manager include:

Financial Analysis and Planning — This involves organizing and using accounting data to monitor the firm's financial condition. It also involves evaluating the need for capital expenditures and determining what additional financing is needed.

Managing the firm's asset structure — This involves managing the firm's cash, marketable securities portfolio, accounts receivable, inventory, equipment and physical plant.

Managing the firm's financial structure — This involves decisions on how assets are financed, use of short-term versus long-term debt, leasing and use of debt versus equity.

1.3 THE ORGANIZATION OF THE FINANCE FUNCTION

Accounting departments typically handle the finance function in small firms. In large firms, there is typically a **Vice President Finance**, or **Chief Financial Officer** (CFO) who reports directly to the President (CEO). Typically, the treasurer and the controller will report to the Vice President Finance.

The **treasurer** is normally responsible for handling financial planning and fund raising, managing cash, capital budgeting analysis, credit and collections and investing of excess funds.

The **controller** normally is responsible for all accounting activities, including tax management, data processing and cost and financial accounting.

1.4 GOALS OF THE FIRM

The broad goal of the firm should be an attempt to maximize the wealth of the firm's present shareholders, if this is a corporation, or the wealth of the firm's owners in a proprietary or partnership organization.

Many times, managers in a corporation are given incentives such as stock options and bonuses to maximize shareholders' wealth. In a proprietary ownership, the owner/manager can benefit directly from profits which can result in bonuses.

Wealth maximization is not inconsistent with social responsibility. Social responsibility will be broadly defined as quality product and service to the firm's customers, concern for employees — a safe working environment and a trained and loyal workforce — and community concern. Because of competitive pressures, government regulation may be needed to protect the responsible firms from the irresponsible firms. Pension funds and mutual funds with a concern about social issues are increasingly having an impact on firms in their role as large shareholders.

CHAPTER 2

BUSINESS ORGANIZATION AND THE FINANCIAL ENVIRONMENT

2.1 BASIC FORMS OF BUSINESS ORGANIZATION

A **proprietorship** is a business owned by one individual. About 75% of all businesses in the U.S. are proprietorships.

The advantages of a proprietorship are:

1. Low cost and ease of formation. No legal documents need be prepared and a state charter is not required.
2. Decisions do not require consent of others.
3. Income tax may be an advantage or disadvantage.

The disadvantages of a proprietorship are:

1. Unlimited liability. Proprietor is personally responsible for all business debts.
2. Difficuly in raising large amounts of capital.

A **partnership** is owned by two or more individuals. Nine percent of all business firms in the U.S. are partnerships.

The advantages of a partnership are:

1. Low cost and ease of formation.
2. Can raise more capital than proprietorship.
3. Can attract talent easier than a proprietorship.
4. Income tax may be an advantage or disadvantage.

The disadvantages of a partnership are:

1. Unlimited liability for each partner. If one partner is unable to pay his or her share, the remaining partner or partners are liable for all business debts. However, limited partnerships have general and limited partners. Limited partners do not participate in management and are liable only for the amount of their invested capital.

2. Difficulty in raising large amounts of capital.

A **corporation** is a legal entity created by a state and is separate and distinct from its owners and managers. Corporations comprise only 16% of all businesses in the U.S., but receive 88% of business receipts and 78% of net profits.

The advantages of a corporation are:

1. Limited liability. Stockholders' liability is limited to their investment; however, in small corporations, officers or major stockholders may be required to personally guarantee a loan.

2. Unlimited life. Shares can be resold.

3. Ability to raise large amounts of money.

4. Salaries and benefits are tax-deductible expenses.

The disadvantages of a corporation are:

1. Time and cost of organizing.

2. Double taxation may be a disadvantage.

A **Subchapter S Corporation** is a special corporation with a limited number of shareholders. An S Corporation is frequently used for a family corporation. An S Corporation is like a regular corporation *except* that it is taxed like a partnership. This is useful in tax planning.

2.2 THE FEDERAL INCOME TAX SYSTEM

A corporation must pay federal income tax on its corporate income.

A corporation's taxable income is calculated by deducting from revenue all expenses, including depreciation and interest.

The tax rates for corporate income are as follows:

0 – $50,000	15%
$50,000 – $75,000	25%
$75,000 – $100,000	34%
$100,000 – $335,000	39%

$335,000 – $10,000,000	34%
$10,000,000 – $15,000,000	35%
$15,000,000 – $18,333,333	38%
$18,333,334 ++++	35%

Average tax rates are found by dividing the taxes owed by taxable income.

Marginal tax rate is the rate applied to the last dollar of taxable income.

Proprietorships, partnerships and S corporations are taxed as personal income.

Personal taxable income is equal to adjusted gross income less personal exemptions and deductions.

There are four tax brackets, with tax rates of 15%, 28%, 33% and 28%. The size of the tax bracket varies with single or family status. This is illustrated below:

Single		**Married (Filing Jointly)**	
Taxable Income	**Marginal Rate**	**Taxable Income**	**Marginal Rate**
0 – $26,250	15%	0 – $43,850	15%
$26,250 – $63,550	28%	$43,850 – $105,950	28%
$63,550 – $132,600	31%	$105,950 – $161,450	31%
$132,600 – $288,350	36%	$161,450 – $288,350	36%
$288,350 ++++	39.6%	$288,350 ++++	39.6%

2.3   FINANCIAL INSTITUTIONS

Financial institutions are intermediaries that channel the savings of individuals, businesses and governments into loans or investments.

The major financial institutions are as follows:

1. **Commercial banks** accept demand and savings accounts, and loan the money to governments, businesses and individuals. They are by far the most important source of loan funds to businesses.

2. **Mutual savings banks** are similar to commercial banks except they cannot offer demand deposits. Mutual saving banks offer savings, NOW and money market accounts and lend money through financial

markets and real estate loans.

3. **Savings and loans** offers savings, NOW and money market accounts, and loans to individuals and businesses for real estate mortgages.

4. **Credit unions** are member organizations in which members usually share some common bond, such as working for the same firm, etc. They offer savings, NOW and money market accounts and loans, to members for automobile, appliances, home improvements or personal needs.

5. **Life insurance companies** receive premiums from individuals for future benefit payments. These are long-term contracts that create large reserves for investing. Funds are loaned to individuals and businesses and in the financial markets.

6. **Pension funds** accumulate money from individuals and employers to pay retirement benefits. They usually invest or loan through the financial markets. They are the largest institutional investor in corporate stocks.

7. **Mutual funds** pool funds of savers and invest them in debt and equity of businesses and government debt.

2.4   FINANCIAL MARKETS

Financial markets provide a forum where savers and users of funds are brought together. There are many financial markets — both geographical and by type of financial activity.

Money markets are the markets for short-term funds — one year or less.

Capital markets are the markets for intermediate and long-term funds — over one year.

Primary markets are markets where funds are provided to the users — a new-issue market.

Secondary markets are resale markets where one investor sells to another investor.

2.5   MONEY MARKETS

Marketable securities are traded in the money markets. The money market is an impersonal market and marketable securities trade on the basis of price and risk. They typically trade in lots of $100,000 or more.

Examples of marketable securities are treasury bills, negotiable CD's, and bankers acceptances. Commercial paper is usually categorized as a marketable security even though the specific issue may not be marketable.

Participants in the money market are typically government securities dealers, business firms, large commercial banks, the Federal Reserve System and other large financial institutions.

2.6 CAPITAL MARKETS

Key securities in the capital markets are bonds, preferred stock and common stocks.

Bonds are long-term debt instruments. There are many types of bonds with different risk characteristics. Bonds have priority over all equity issues.

Preferred stocks are equity (ownership interest) with preference over common stock. They usually have a fixed return and are non-voting.

Common stocks are equity and have no fixed return. They usually have voting privileges.

Securities exchanges create continuous markets and thus give liquidity, allocate scarce capital, determine and publicize security prices, and aid in new financing.

Organized exchanges have a physical location and use the auction process. They involve only the secondary market.

Over two-thirds of all shares traded are traded on organized exchanges. The New York Stock Exchange has over 80% of shares traded by volume on organized exchanges. Shares are also traded on the American Stock Exchange and several regional stock exchanges.

The Over-the-Counter Exchange (OTC) is a nationwide network linked by sophisticated telecommunications. Market makers buy and sell from inventory; prices are determined by competitive bid and negotiation. The OTC deals both in the primary and secondary market.

2.7 INTEREST RATES AND REQUIRED RETURNS

The **real rate of interest** is the interest rate which would prevail in the absence of risk and inflationary expectations. The real rate is determined solely by supply and demand for funds.

The **actual or nominal rate of interest** is the rate paid in the market, equal to the real interest rate plus risk adjustment plus inflation adjustment plus liquidity preference.

Investors and lenders require a higher rate of return for assuming risk. This is called a **risk premium**. There are three elements of the risk premium. They are:

1. **Default risk** — the risk that a loan or investment will not be repaid.

2. **Maturity risk** — when interest rates rise, bond prices fall. The greater the years to maturity, the greater the change in price.

3. **Marketability risk** — the more highly marketable the issue, the lower the risk.

Other features, such as tax treatment of the interest and contractual provisions (e.g., freely callable, subordinated) influence the interest rates.

The yield curve reflects liquidity preferences of investors and lenders. It is a graph of yields of securities of different maturities — usually U.S. Treasury securities. Normally, the yield curve slopes upward to the right (A). If inflation is expected to decrease, the yield curve may slope downward to the right (B).

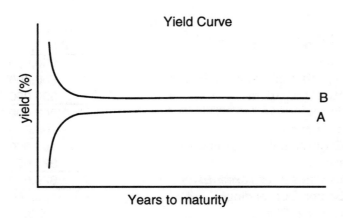

CHAPTER 3

FINANCIAL STATEMENTS, DEPRECIATION AND CASH FLOW

3.1 INCOME STATEMENT

The income statement measures the profitability of the firm over a specific time frame. A simple income statement is shown below.

Ace Corporation
Income Statement
For the Year Ended December 31, 20XX

Sales	$ 10,000,000
Cost of Goods Sold	8,000,000
Gross Profits	2,000,000
Selling and Administrative Expense	500,000
Depreciation Expense	300,000
Operating Profit (EBIT)	1,200,000
Interest Expense	100,000
Earnings before Taxes (EBT)	1,100,000
Taxes	374,000
Earnings After Taxes (EAT)	$ 626,000
Shares Outstanding	100,000
Earnings per Share	$ 6.26

Note that the income statement covers a **period of time**, in this case, January 1 – December 31, 20XX. The earnings after taxes may be paid as dividends to stockholders or reinvested in the firm. If reinvested, they are called retained earnings.

3.2 BALANCE SHEET

The balance sheet (Statement of Financial Position) shows what a firm owns (assets) and how these assets were financed through borrowing (liabilities) and owner money (equity). The balance sheet reflects the financial position **at a moment in time,** not a period of time. A simple comparative balance sheet is shown on the following page.

3.3 ANALYZING THE FIRM'S FUNDS FLOWS

Sources and uses of funds is a worksheet which explains where funds were used during any accounting period and how these funds were generated. See Table on Page 13.

A **source** of funds is any decrease in an asset, an increase in a liability or an increase in an equity account.

A **use** of funds is any increase in an asset, a decrease in a liabiity or a decrease in an equity account.

A "quick and dirty" sources and uses worksheet is prepared by classifying the changes between the two years on a comparative balance sheet.

Sources and uses must balance. If they do not, either an account was incorrectly classified or the balance sheets do not balance.

An important adjustment to the sources and uses worksheet involves retained earnings. According to the worksheet example, retained earnings increased by $500,000. Referring to the Ace Corporation income statement, earnings after taxes were $626,000. The sources and uses should be adjusted by replacing retained earnings ($500,000) as a source with earnings after taxes ($626,000) and a use of dividends ($126,000).

The Sources and Uses worksheet is usually reorganized into the form below and called a Sources and Uses statement.

Ace Corporation
Statement of Financial Position
For the Year Ended December 31

Assets		20X1		20X0
Current Assets				
Cash		$ 100,000		$ 50,000
Marketable Securities		1,100,000		1,800,000
Accounts Receivable, less allowance				
for uncollectable accounts of $50,000				
(19X9) and $40,000 (19 X8)		1,200,000		1,000,000
Inventory		1,500,000		1,100,000
Prepaid Expenses		100,000		100,000
Total Current Assets		4,000,000		4,050,000
Other Assets				
Investments		500,000		– 0 –
Fixed Assets				
Equipment	1,000,000		500,000	
Buildings	2,000,000		1,000,000	
Less Accumulated				
Depreciation	500,000	2,500,000	300,000	1,200,000
Land		1,000,000		550,000
		$8,000,000		$5,800,000

Liabilities and Stockholders Equity	20X1	20X0
Current Liabilities		
Accounts Payable	$ 250,000	$ 200,000
Current Maturity on Mortgage	100,000	– 0 –
Accrued Expenses	150,000	100,000
Total Current Liabilites	500,000	300,000
Long-term Liabilities		
Mortgage	1,500,000	– 0 –
Total Liabilities	2,000,000	300,000
Stockholders' Equity		
Common Stock, $1 par value;		
100,000 shares	100,000	100,000
Capital Paid in Excess of Par	2,900,000	2,900,000
Retained Earnings	3,000,000	2,500,000
Total Stockholders' Equity	6,000,000	5,500,000
Total Liabilities and Stockholders'		
Equity	$8,000,000	$5,800,000

The financial statements above will be used in the following section on Analyzing the firm's funds flows and in Chapter 4, Financial Statement Analysis.

Sources and Uses
Ace Corporation, 20X0–20X1

	Sources	Uses
Cash		$ 50,000
Marketable Securities	$ 700,000	
Accounts Receivable		200,000
Inventory		400,000
Investments		500,000
Equipment		500,000
Buildings		1,000,000
Depreciation	200,000	
Land		450,000
Accounts Payable	50,000	
Current Maturities, L.T. Debt	100,000	
Accrued Expenses	50,000	
Mortgage	1,500,000	
Retained Earnings	500,000	
	$3,100,000	$3,100,000

Sources		Uses	
Marketable Securities	$700,000	Cash	$ 50,000
Depreciation	200,000	Accounts Receivable	200,000
Accounts Payable	50,000	Inventory	400,000
Current Maturities,		Investments	500,000
L.T. Debt	100,000	Equipment	500,000
Accrued Expenses	50,000	Buildings	1,000,000
Mortgage	1,500,000	Land	450,000
Earnings after Taxes	626,000	Dividends	126,000
	$3,226,000		$3,226,000

Some finance authors label the above statement the Cash Flow Statement or Statement of Changes in Financial Position. Accountants, and a few finance authors, use the following form for the Statement of Cash Flows.

Statement of Cash Flows
For the Year Ended December 31, 20XX

Cash provided (Used) by Operations:	
Net income	$ 626,000
Income charges (credits) not affecting cash:	
Depreciation	200,000
Changes in certain working capital components:	
Increase in inventory	(400,000)
Increase in accounts receivable	(200,000)
Increase in accounts payable	50,000
Increase in accrued expenses	50,000
Cash provided by operations	326,000
Cash provided (used by investing activities) :	
Additions to property, plant and equipment	(1,950,000)
Additions to Investments	(500,000)
Cash used by investing activities	(2,450,000)
Cash provided (used) by financing activities:	
Additions to long-term debt including current portion	1,600,000
Dividends	(126,000)
Cash provided by financing activities	1,474,000
Net increase (decrease) in cash and equivalents	(650,000)
Cash and equivalents, beginning of year	$1,850,000
Cash and equivalents, end of year	$1,200,000

3.4   DEPRECIATION

The Tax Reform Act of 1986, and the many revisions from that point onward, provides for various forms of depreciation, and many rules within each classification. For tax purposes, the method that maximizes the depreciation deduction would normally be used.

First, there is the Section 179 Deduction which allows a business to deduct all or part of the cost of qualifying equipment in the year it was put in service. Next, there is the Modified Accelerated Cost Recovery System (MACRS) which has several parts:

1. The 200% declining balance method.
2. The 150% declining balance method.
3. The Straight Line Method which is the cost of the item depreciated equally over the defined life of the item.
4. The Alternative Depreciation System (ADS) under which certain items such as tax exempt property can be depreciated.

The Internal Revenue Service publishes in specific detail, all of the rules, exceptions, and illustrations of the various applications of Depreciation. It is called Publication 946.

Property class (Recovery period)	Definition
3-year	Research and experiment equipment and certain special tools.
5-year	Computers, typewriters, copiers, duplicating equipment, cars, light-duty trucks, qualified technological equipment, and similar assets.
7-year	Office furniture, fixtures, most manufacturing equipment, railroad track, and single-purpose agricultural and horticultural structures.
10-year	Equipment used in petroleum refining or in the manufacture of tobacco products and certain food products.

Depreciation is a **non-cash expense**. It is a **source of funds** because the cash outflow occurs at the time of purchase and is then amortized over the life of the asset by including it as an expense in product pricing. Including depreciation as a non-cash expense serves as a **tax shield** by reducing taxable net income.

CHAPTER 4

FINANCIAL STATEMENTS ANALYSIS

4.1 BASIC TYPES OF FINANCIAL RATIOS

Different finance authors use different classification systems for describing financial ratios. One common system is the four categories of ratios used in this chapter. Examples of ratio calculations will use Ace Corporation data from Chapter 3.

4.1.1 LIQUIDITY RATIOS

The most common liquidity ratios are the **current ratio** and the **quick ratio** (acid test ratio). **Net working capital**, while not a ratio, is a measure of liquidity and frequently included in this section. The inventory valuation method can have a significant impact on current ratio and net working capital.

Current Ratio — Current assets ÷ current liabilities.

$4,000,000 ÷ 500,000 = 8:1 current ratio

Quick Ratio — Strictly speaking, "quick" assets are cash, marketable securities and accounts receivable. Usually, however, the quick ratio is calculated as current assets less inventory ÷ current liabilities.

$4,000,000 − 1,500,000 ÷ 500,000 = 5:1 quick ratio

Net Working Capital — Current assets − current liabilities.

$4,000,000 − 500,000 = $3,500,000 net working capital

4.1.2 ACTIVITY RATIOS

Activity ratios, frequently called turnover ratios, are considered good measures of management effectiveness. In particular, management can

16

directly affect inventory and accounts receivable ratios which short-term creditors will examine. If a firm has difficulty paying bills when due (liquidity), activity ratios affecting working capital will be closely examined.

Inventory Turnover — Inventory turnover seeks to determine if inventory is excessive or has been changing significantly. It is usually measured as cost of goods sold divided by inventory (or average inventory). Inventory valuation methods significantly affect this ratio.

(Inventory)

$$\$8,000,000 \div 1,500,000 = 5.33 \text{ times}$$

or

(avg. inventory)

$$\$8,000,000 \div 1,300,000 = 6.15 \text{ times}$$

Sometimes, inventory turnover is calculated by sales divided by inventory (or average inventory).

(Inventory)

$$\$10,000,000 \div 1,500,000 = 6.67 \text{ times}$$

or

(avg. inventory)

$$\$10,000,000 \div 1,300,000 = 7.69 \text{ times}$$

Obviously, when comparing with published industry data (cross section analysis), it is important to determine what method is used in calculating the published data.

Accounts Receivable Turnover — Accounts receivable turnover seeks to determine if credit allowed by the firm is excessive. Accounts receivable is an interest-free loan from the buyer to the seller and requires financing by the buyer.

sales ÷ accounts receivable or average accounts receivable

$$\$10,000,000 \div 1,200,000 = 8.33 \text{ times}$$

or

$$\$10,000,000 \div 1,100,000 = 9.09 \text{ times}$$

A more commonly used but similar measure is average days outstanding of receivables.

$$\text{sales} \div 360 = \text{sales per day}$$

Average Days Outstanding — Accounts receivable ÷ by sales per day

$$\$10,000,000 \div 360 = 27,777.78$$

$$\$1,200,000 \div 27,777.78 = 43.2 \text{ days}$$

Note that 8.33 times (accounts receivable turnover) divided into 360 days = 43.22 days.

Fixed Asset Turnover — Fixed asset turnover seeks to determine if investment in fixed assets is excessive. The age of assets, depreciation policies and use of leases all impact this ratio.

$$\text{sales} \div \text{fixed assets (or average fixed assets)}$$

$$\$10,000,000 \div 2,500,000 = 4 \text{ times}$$

or

$$\$10,000,000 \div 1,850,000 = 5.41 \text{ times}$$

Total Asset Turnover: Sales ÷ total assets (or average total assets)

$$\$10,000,000 \div 8,000,000 = 1.25$$

or

$$\$10,000,000 \div 6,900,000 = 1.45$$

4.1.3 DEBT RATIOS

Degree of indebtedness ratios can be readily calculated by the external analyst. These ratios focus on the amount of loan principal and ignore the impact of interest rates.

Debt Ratio — Total liabilities ÷ total assets

$$\$2,000,000 \div 8,000,000 = 25\%$$

Debt-Equity Ratios — This ratio focuses on capital structure rather than the financial structure as reflected in the debt ratio. Different authors calculate this ratio differently. Both methods are shown below:

1. Long-term debt ÷ stockholders equity

$$\$1,500,000 \div 6,000,000 = 25\%$$

2. Long-term debt to total capitalization

$$\text{long-term debt} \div \text{long-term debt} + \text{equity}$$

$$\$1,500,000 \div 7,500,000 = 20\%$$

Ability to Service Debt — These ratios recognize the varying burden faced by the firm during periods of high interest rates versus low interest rates. This is not reflected by degree of indebtedness ratios.

Times Interest Earned Ratio — Earnings before interest and taxes (EBIT) ÷ total interest

$$\$1,200,000 \div 100,000 = 12 \text{ times}$$

Fixed Payment Coverage Ratio — Earnings before interest and taxes (EBIT) ÷ interest plus principal payments and preferred dividends adjusted to before-taxes amount.

4.1.4 PROFITABILITY RATIOS

Profitability ratios are of particular interest to investors and long-term creditors. Long-term debt is repaid from earnings.

Gross Profit Margin — This represents the excess of sales over cost of goods.

$$\text{gross profit} \div \text{sales}$$
$$\$2,000,000 \div \$10,000,000 = 20\%$$

Operating Profit Margin — This ratio looks at the operating efficiency of the firm by ignoring interest on debt and non-operating activities.

$$\text{operating profit (EBIT)} \div \text{sales}$$
$$\$1,200,000 \div \$10,000,000 = 12\%$$

The following four ratios compare net profit after tax to various bases.

Net Profit Margin — Net profit after tax ÷ sales

$$\$626,000 \div \$10,000,000 = 6.26\%$$

Return on Investment (ROI) — Net profit after tax ÷ total assets

$$\$626,000 \div \$8,000,000 = 7.83\%$$

Return on Equity (ROE) — Net profit after tax ÷ total equity

$$\$626,000 \div \$6,000,000 = 10.43\%$$

Earnings Per Share (EPS) — Net profit after tax ÷ common shares

$$\$626,000 \div 100,000 = \$6.26$$

4.2   CROSS SECTION ANALYSIS

Cross section analysis compares the firm under study with average data from comparable firms. These comparable firms' data, or industry averages, are available from several sources. Among the best known sources of industry average data are Robert Morris Associates (commercial bank lending officers) and Dun and Bradstreet. National accounting firms and industry trade associations compile industry data.

4.3   TREND ANALYSIS

Trend analysis compares the current year financial data with previous years' data. Comparative ratios, common size financial statements and percentage changes are the principal methods used for trend analysis.

4.4   DUPONT SYSTEM OF ANALYSIS

DuPont developed a system of analysis for internal operating control using control charts. As developed and used by DuPont, it can be used for various subdivisions of the company. The form they developed for internal control purpose is:

$$\frac{\text{operating profit}}{\text{sales}} \times \frac{\text{sales}}{\text{operating assets}} = \text{Return on Investment (ROI)}$$

Most finance books use a modified form of the DuPont Analysis, as shown below:

$$\frac{\text{net profit after taxes}}{\text{sales}} \times \frac{\text{sales}}{\text{total assets}} = (\text{ROI})$$

The above uses the ratios from section 4.1 and states the net profit margin times total asset turnover equals return on investment.

The complete DuPont system involves analysis of the individual ratios comprising the profit margin and turnover. In addition, it can be modified to calculate ROE. A more complete version is shown on the following page.

As shown in the diagram following, net profit margin could be analyzed by calculating its parts, such as gross profit margin, selling expense ÷ sales, administrative expense ÷ sales, operating profit margin, etc. In a similar way, total asset turnover could be analyzed by calculating turn-

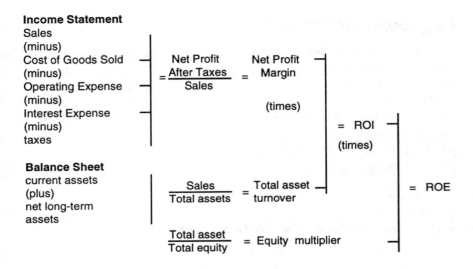

Income Statement
Sales
(minus)
Cost of Goods Sold
(minus)
Operating Expense
(minus)
Interest Expense
(minus)
taxes

$= \dfrac{\text{Net Profit After Taxes}}{\text{Sales}} = $ Net Profit Margin

(times)

= ROI

(times)

Balance Sheet
current assets
(plus)
net long-term
assets

$\dfrac{\text{Sales}}{\text{Total assets}} = $ Total asset turnover

= ROE

$\dfrac{\text{Total asset}}{\text{Total equity}} = $ Equity multiplier

over for each category of assets. The DuPont system uses this approach of charting these individual ratios at regular intervals to detect undesirable trends that will affect ROI. The chart also shows that the extended version of Return on Investment (ROI) times the Equity multiplier equals Return on Equity (ROE).

4.5   SOME LIMITATIONS OF RATIO ANALYSIS

While Ratio Analysis may be limited by the quality of data (influenced by variables such as accounting, inflation, seasonal differences affecting trend and cross-section analysis), managers have a continuing need to make decisions within a reasonable time, without having to wait for all the variables to be resolved. Pristine accuracy in critical management situations is not always required.

Ratio analysis remains an effective business method by comparing functions within a business to guide management in making the business profitable by detecting a loss situation, defining sales growth, production efficiency, and controlling the number of employees used.

CHAPTER 5

FINANCIAL PLANNING

5.1 THE FINANCIAL PLANNING PROCESS

The financial planning process begins with long run, or strategic, financial plans. These plans incorporate planned expansions, research and development efforts, acquisitions or other planned actions and major sources of financing.

The planning horizon will vary among industries depending upon the operating uncertainties; however, five-year strategic financial plans are common.

Short run, or operating, financial plans for the year ahead are developed within the framework of the strategic financial plan.

The components of an operating financial plan are listed below:

Budgeted (Pro forma) Income Statement

Sales budget

Costs-of-goods-sold budget

Production budget

Direct materials purchases budget

Direct labor cost budget

Factory overhead cost budget

Operating expenses budget (may consist of several budgets)

Budgeted (Pro forma) Balance Sheet

Capital Expenditures Budget

Cash Budget

Financial managers work with the pro forma income statement, cash budget, capital expenditures budget (see Chapter 10) and the pro forma balance sheet.

The accuracy of the sales forecast is the key to the budgeted financial statements. Most of the components of the pro forma statements are based upon the sales forecast.

Sales forecasts are prepared in various ways. They are sometimes classified as external (or top-down) forecasts and internal (bottom-up) forecasts.

The external forecast is based on relationships between the firm's sales and various economic indicators involving the firm's sales area. Sophisticated econometric models may be used or less sophisticated regression or trend analysis may be used.

The internal (bottom-up) forecast may start with individual forecasts by salespeople for their territory. These are aggregated and adjusted by sales managers and a consensus forecast developed. The external and internal forecasts are then reconciled.

5.2 PRO FORMA INCOME STATEMENT

A Pro Forma Income Statement starts with the sales forecast and may be prepared for whatever time intervals are desired. For example, monthly, quarterly, or semiannual statements may be desired.

Costs of goods sold and operating expenses budgets provide the data for the pro forma income statement.

After-tax earnings from this statement are used to determine retained earnings on the balance sheet.

5.3 THE CASH BUDGET

The cash budget forecasts the **cash** that will be received and disbursed during various time periods in the future. Large firms may do a daily cash forecast for the first week, then weekly cash forecasts for the following three weeks, then monthly forecasts for the remainder of the year.

There are many formats used for cash budgets. The first section is typically cash receipts. Cash receipts consist of all cash sales, collection of accounts receivable and all non-operating cash receipts.

Cash disbursements follow cash receipts and include all cash payments — purchases, expenses, interest, debt repayment, capital equipment payments and dividends.

Total receipts minus disbursements equals net cash inflow or outflow. This is added to the beginning cash balance to determine ending cash. Funds must be borrowed if necessary to return cash to the desired level. This becomes next period's beginning cash.

A cash budget (budgeted statement of cash receipts and disbursements) is shown on the following page.

The cash budget shows amount and timing of borrowing needed and when and how the money can be repaid. The cash budget also shows the amount of excess funds available for investing and the period of time the excess funds are available.

5.4 PRO FORMA BALANCE SHEET

The budgeted (pro forma) balance sheet uses the cash balance from the cash budget and accounts receivable derived from the sales budget and used in the cash budget. Inventory and accounts payable are derived from the production budget. Plant and equipment is derived from the capital expenditure budget and the depreciation schedule. Bank loans, other borrowing and new equity financing are shown on the cash budget. Additions to retained earnings are derived from the income statement.

Pro forma balance sheets are typically projected annually for the next five years to study longer run financing needs in order to develop financial strategy. For strategic planning, the detailed budgets, including the cash budget, would be omitted. The pro forma income statement and pro forma balance sheet would be prepared using trend analysis modified by the strategic plan.

ACE CORPORATION
Budgeted Statement of Cash Receipts and Disbursements
For The Two Months Ended June 30, 20X0

	May	June
Cash balance, beginning	50,000	178,333
Cash receipts		
Cash sales	90,000	110,000
Collection of accounts receivable	900,000	810,000
Total cash available for needs,		
before financing	1,040,000	1,098,333
Cash disbursements		
Purchases	720,000	880,000
Selling and administrative expense	41,667	41,667
Dividends		20,000
Equipment purchases	100,000	200,000
Total Disbursements	861,667	1,141,667
Minimum cash balance desired	50,000	50,000
Total cash needed	911,667	1,191,667
Excess (deficiency) of total cash		
available over total cash		
needed before current financing	128,333	(93,334)
Financing		
Borrowings (at beginning)	—	93,334
Repayments (at ends)	—	—
Interest (at 12% per annum)	—	—
Total cash increase (decrease) from		
financing	—	93,334
Cash balance, ending	178,333	50,000

CHAPTER 6

OPERATING AND FINANCIAL LEVERAGE

6.1 OPERATING LEVERAGE

Leverage results from the use of fixed-cost assets to finance borrowing that will ultimately be used to increase profits. Organizations use leverage to avoid the use of cash reserves that may be tied up in an intermediate or long-term project.

6.1.1 BREAK-EVEN ANALYSIS

Break-even analysis, called cost-volume-profit analysis in accounting texts, is used for studying the level of sales needed to cover all costs. This is useful in analyzing the purchase of either assets or an entire business. It is also helpful in analyzing profitability levels of the entire operation, or of specific products in a multi-product line.

Break-even analysis requires that costs be analyzed and classified as fixed costs or variable costs. In practice, fixed costs are only fixed over some relevant range of output and for a finite time period. Variable costs are assumed to vary directly with sales at a constant rate. While these assumptions may not be exactly correct, they usually are adequate for most decision purposes.

In the algebraic approach to break-even analysis, the formula below is used to calculate the quantity of units that must be sold to exactly break-even — no profit, no loss.

$$Q = \frac{FC}{P - VC}$$

where Q = Break-even Quantity

FC = Total Fixed Cost
P = Unit Price
VC = Unit Variable Cost

$P - VC$ in the above equation results in the "contribution margin," expressed in dollars, per unit.

To calculate the break-even point in total sales rather than quantity, the following formula is used.

$$BE = \frac{FC}{1 - \left(\dfrac{VC}{S}\right)}$$

$1 - (^{VC}/_S)$ is contribution margin expressed as a decimal.

The break-even formula can be extended to calculate cash break-even by subtracting non-cash expenses from the fixed cost. Thus

$$Q - \frac{FC - D}{P - VC}$$

where D = Depreciation Expense.

The break-even formula can also be adjusted to calculate break-even including a desired level of profit. Assume that $50,000 is the desired net profit. Thus:

$$Q = \frac{FC + \$50,000}{P - VC}$$

It is important to remember the limitations of break-even analysis. They are:

1. It assumes constant sales price.

2. It assumes product mix does not change.

3. It assumes variable costs increase linearly with sales.

4. Fixed costs are only fixed over some relevant range.

The graphic approach to break-even analysis is especially useful to demonstrate the risk inherent in the asset structure. As shown below, when sales exceed the break-even level, net profit increases rapidly (positive leverage). When sales fall below the break-even point, net loss increases rapidly (negative leverage). A break-even graph would typically be viewed from the standpoint of pessimistic level of sales, expected level of sales, and optimistic level of sales.

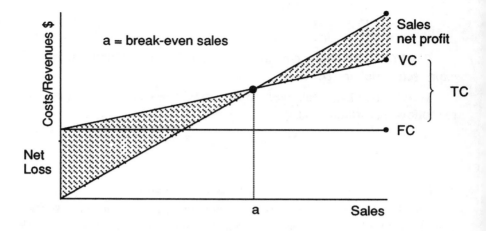

6.1.2 DEGREE OF OPERATING LEVERAGE

The degree of operating leverage (DOL) calculates the rate of change in profits (EBIT), as shown in the break-even chart above, as sales increase or decrease. Assume a DOL of 1.30. This means that profits will increase by 1.3% for each 1% increase of sales past the break-even point. Unfortunately, at sales levels below break-even, losses are magnified in the same manner. The formula for calculating degree of operating leverage (DOL) is shown below:

$$Q = \frac{\% \text{ change in EBIT}}{\% \text{ change in Sales}}$$

6.2 FINANCIAL LEVERAGE

Financial leverage results from the use of fixed-cost financing — debt and preferred stock — to magnify returns to the common equity holders. Financial leverage is analyzed by the use of break-even charts and the degree of financial leverage.

6.2.1 EARNINGS PER SHARE BREAK-EVEN ANALYSIS

To find EPS break-even point, calculate earnings per share (EPS) under two financing alternatives, for example bonds and common equity. Then calculate for two levels of earnings before interest and taxes (EBIT) and plot the points on a graph.

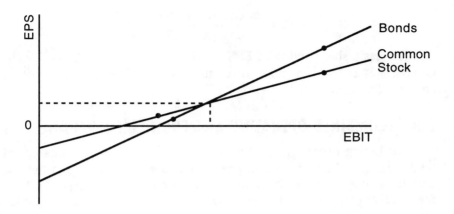

Uncommitted earnings per share (UEPS) break-even analysis uses the calculations for EPS but subtracts debt repayments or sinking fund from earnings after tax. The uncommitted earnings after tax is divided by the number of common shares to calculate UEPS.

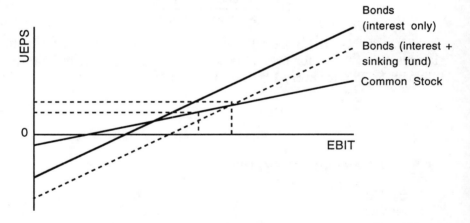

6.2.2 DEGREE OF FINANCIAL LEVERAGE

The degree of financial leverage (DFL) assumes EBIT is given and examines the financial effects of different financial structures on Earnings per Share (EPS). Assume a DFL of 1.25. EPS would increase by 1.25% for each increase of 1% increase in EBIT past the level of break-even sales. Again, leverage works both ways and EPS would fall in the same proportion. The formula for calculating DFL is shown here:

$$DFL = \frac{\% \text{ change in EPS}}{\% \text{ change in EBIT}}$$

The basic shortcoming of EPS – EBIT analysis and DFL is that the emphasis is on maximization of earnings rather than maximization of shareholder wealth.

6.3   COMBINED OPERATING AND FINANCIAL LEVERAGE

Combining operating and financial leverage results in a measure of total leverage. The higher the degree of total leverage, the higher the risk and the higher the potential return. The degree of total leverage (DTL) is the product of operating leverage (DOL) and financial leverage (DFL). Thus:

$$DTL = DOL \times DFL$$

or

$$DTL = \frac{\% \text{ change in EPS}}{\% \text{ change in sales}}$$

Thus, if DOL is 1.3 and DFL is 1.25, then DTL = 1.625 or EPS will increase by 1.625% for every 1.00% increase in sales or EPS will decline by 1.625% for every 1.00% decline in sales.

CHAPTER 7

TIME VALUE OF MONEY

The time value of money underlies all valuation concepts in finance, including capital budgeting and security values. Loan payments, sinking fund payments and other annuity streams are other examples of the use of time value of money.

7.1   FUTURE VALUE (COMPOUND VALUE)

Future-value calculations are involved whenever the unknown sum is in the future. An example is a U.S. Government Series E Savings Bond. The bond is sold at a discounted price and compounds interest at varying rates over the life of the bond. A future-value calculation would yield the value at maturity.

There are two basic tables of future value: The future value of $1 at the end of n periods and the sum of an annuity of $1 per period for n periods.

Future value of $1 tables are used for cashflows of unequal amounts, unequal time periods, or single sums. See Table 1.

Sums of an annuity of $1 per period for n periods tables are used if the cashflows are of equal amounts and equal time periods. See Table 2.

Special purpose tables are frequently constructed from the basic tables. An example is a sinking fund table (deposits to accumulate a future sum). The sinking fund interest factor (SFIF) is calculated by:

$$\frac{1}{FVIFA_{k,n}}$$

See Table 2.

Other future-value formulas:

1) Basic formula:

$$F_n = P \times (1 + k)^n$$

therefore:

$$\text{FVIF} = (1 + k)^n$$

2) Compounding more frequently than annual

$$\text{FVIF} = (1 + \frac{k}{m})^{m \times n}$$

where: m = the number of compounding periods per year.

Assume you have savings of \$1,000 in an account that pays 8% interest, payable quarterly. Assume that you intend to leave the funds in the bank for two years. Thus, using the formula above, we have

$$\text{FVIF} = (1 + \frac{8\%}{4})^{4 \times 2} = 2\%, 8 \text{ periods}$$

using Table 1, 2%, 8 periods, the FVIF is 1.172. Thus, at the end of 2 years, your \$1,000 will grow to \$1,172.

3) Deposits to accumulate a future sum

$$A = \frac{S_n}{\text{FVIFA}_{k,n}}$$

where: A = annual deposit
S_n = future sum

Assume you wish to visit New Zealand and Australia and that you estimate that \$10,000 is needed to make the trip. You plan on departing in 5 years. You believe that you can earn 10% on the deposited funds. Using Table 2, 10%, 5 years is 6.105. The amount you must save each year is shown below:

$$\frac{10,000}{6.105} = \$1,638$$

This is the amount that you would need to deposit each year, earning 20%, in order to have \$10,000 at the end of 5 years.

4) Growth rates (dividends)

$$\frac{D_4}{D_1} = \text{FVIF}_{k,n}$$

Assume the following dividends:

19X2 $1.10
19X3 $1.17
19X4 $1.30
19X5 $1.45
19X6 $1.70

$$\frac{D_5}{D_1} = \frac{1.70}{1.10} = 1.54545_{k,4}$$

$n = 4$ because 4 years elapse between year-end 19X2 and 19X6

Looking at Table 1, 4 years, an FVIF of 1.54545 is between 11% and 12%.

7.2 PRESENT VALUE

Present-value calculations are involved whenever there are cash values occurring in the future and their present equivalent is desired. A bond price is the present value of all future cash flows.

There are two basic tables of present value: The present value of $1 discounted at k percent and the present value of $1 annuity received at the end of n periods at k percent.

Present value of $1 tables are used for single cash flows or cash flows which are of uneven time or amount. See Table 3.

Present value of $1 annuity tables are used for future cash flows that are equal amounts and equal intervals. See Table 4.

Basic present-value formulas are reciprocals of future-value formulas. The basic future-value formula used earlier was $F_n = P \times (1 + k)^n$. P = principal or present value. The reciprocal of this formula is

$$P = \frac{F_n}{(1+k)^n} = F_n \times [\frac{1}{1+k^n}].$$

Therefore the basic formula for

$$PVIF_{k,n} = \frac{1}{1+k^n}.$$

Loan amortization tables such as a mortgage, are constructed using the present value of annuity table. Loan amortization interest factor

$$(LAIF) = \frac{1}{PVIFA_{k,n}}$$

33

Other present-value formulas:

1) Basic formula

$$PVIF_{k,n} = \frac{1}{(1+k)^n}$$

2) Present value of an annuity

$$PVIFA_{k,n} = \sum_{t=1}^{n} \frac{1}{(1+k)^t}$$

3) Loan amortization

$$A = \frac{P_n}{PVIFA_{k,n}}$$

where A = annual payment

Assume you wish to negotiate a 5-year term loan, $100,000 principal, 12% interest, amortized annually. Your annual level payment is:

$$\frac{\$100,000}{3.605} = \$27,739.25$$

Assume the bank requires quarterly payments. Using the concept in "compounding more frequently than annual," $k = 12\% \div 4 = 3\%$ and $n = 4 \times 5 = 20$ periods. Thus the quarterly payment is:

$$\frac{\$100,000}{14.878} = \$6,721.33$$

4) To find an interest rate

$$\frac{P}{A} = PVIFA_{k,n}$$

where P = principal
         A = annual payment

Assume you borrow $1,000 and are asked to repay $500 per year for 3 years. The interest rate is calculated by:

$$\frac{1.000}{\$500} = 2.0$$

referring to Table 4, 3 years, the interest rate is between 20% and 25%.

5) Growth rate (dividends)

$$\frac{D_1}{D_4} = PVIF_{k,n}$$

Using the earlier example under future values,

$$\frac{D_1}{D_5} = \frac{1.10}{1.70} = .647_{k,4}$$

Using table 3, 4 years, we find k is between 11% and 12%.

A **perpetuity** is a special form of present value that assumes a cash flow forever. If the cash flow is level, the following formula applies:

$$P = \frac{A}{k}$$

where A = annual payment
               k = market rate of interest

Assume a perpetuity bond pays $100 per year in perpetuity and the present market rate of interest is 12%. The bond price would then be:

$$\frac{\$100}{.12} = \$833.33$$

TABLE 1 — Future-Value Interest Factors for One Dollar Compounded at k Percent for n Periods: $\text{FVIF}_{k,n} = (1 + k)^n$

Period	1%	2%	3%	4%	5%	6%	7%	8%	9%	10%	11%	12%	13%	14%	15%	16%	20%	25%	30%	35%
1	1.010	1.020	1.030	1.040	1.050	1.060	1.070	1.080	1.090	1.100	1.110	1.120	1.130	1.140	1.150	1.160	1.200	1.250	1.300	1.350
2	1.020	1.040	1.061	1.082	1.102	1.124	1.145	1.166	1.188	1.210	1.232	1.254	1.277	1.300	1.322	1.346	1.440	1.562	1.690	1.822
3	1.030	1.061	1.093	1.125	1.158	1.191	1.225	1.260	1.295	1.331	1.368	1.405	1.443	1.482	1.521	1.561	1.728	1.953	2.197	2.460
4	1.041	1.082	1.126	1.170	1.216	1.262	1.311	1.360	1.412	1.464	1.518	1.574	1.630	1.689	1.749	1.811	2.074	2.441	2.856	3.321
5	1.051	1.104	1.159	1.217	1.276	1.338	1.403	1.469	1.539	1.611	1.685	1.762	1.842	1.925	2.011	2.100	2.488	3.052	3.713	4.484
6	1.062	1.126	1.194	1.265	1.340	1.419	1.501	1.587	1.677	1.772	1.870	1.974	2.082	2.195	2.313	2.436	2.986	3.815	4.827	6.053
7	1.072	1.149	1.230	1.316	1.407	1.504	1.606	1.714	1.828	1.949	2.076	2.211	2.353	2.502	2.660	2.826	3.583	4.768	6.275	8.172
8	1.083	1.172	1.267	1.369	1.477	1.594	1.718	1.851	1.993	2.144	2.305	2.476	2.658	2.853	3.059	3.278	4.300	5.960	8.157	11.032
9	1.094	1.195	1.305	1.423	1.551	1.689	1.838	1.999	2.172	2.358	2.558	2.773	3.004	3.252	3.518	3.803	5.160	7.451	10.604	14.894
10	1.105	1.219	1.344	1.480	1.629	1.791	1.967	2.159	2.367	2.594	2.839	3.106	3.395	3.707	4.046	4.411	6.192	9.313	13.786	20.106
11	1.116	1.243	1.384	1.539	1.710	1.898	2.105	2.332	2.580	2.853	3.152	3.479	3.836	4.226	4.652	5.117	7.430	11.642	17.921	27.144
12	1.127	1.268	1426	1.601	1.796	2.012	2.252	2.518	2.813	3.138	3.498	3.896	4.334	4.818	5.350	5.936	8.916	14.552	23.298	36.644
13	1.138	1.294	1.469	1.665	1.886	2.133	2.410	2.720	3.066	3.452	3.883	4.363	4.898	5.492	6.153	6.886	10.699	18.190	30.287	49.469
14	1.149	1.319	1.513	1.732	1.980	2.261	2.579	2.937	3.342	3.797	4.310	4.887	5.535	6.261	7.076	7.987	12.839	22.737	39.373	66.784
15	1.161	1.346	1.558	1.801	2.079	2.397	2.759	3.172	3.642	4.177	4.785	5.474	6.254	7.138	8.137	9.265	15.407	28.422	51.185	90.158
16	1.173	1.373	1.605	1.873	2.183	2.540	2.952	3.426	3.970	4.595	5.311	6.130	7.067	8.137	9.358	10.748	18.488	35.527	66.541	121.71
17	1.184	1.400	1.653	1.948	2.292	2.693	3.159	3.700	4.328	5.054	5.895	6.866	7.986	9.276	10.761	12.468	22.186	44.409	86.503	164.31
18	1.196	1.428	1.702	2.026	2.407	2.854	3.380	3.996	4.717	5.560	6.543	7.690	9.024	10.575	12.375	14.462	26.623	55.511	112.45	221.82
19	1.208	1.457	1.753	2.107	2.527	3.026	3.616	4.316	5.142	6.116	7.263	8.613	10.197	12.055	14.232	16.776	31.948	69.389	146.19	299.46
20	1.220	1.486	1.806	2.191	2.653	3.207	3.870	4.661	5.604	6.727	8.062	9.646	11.523	13.743	16.366	19.461	38.337	86.736	190.05	404.27
21	1.232	1.516	1.860	2.279	2.786	3.399	4.140	5.034	6.109	7.400	8.949	10.804	13.021	15.667	18.821	22.574	46.005	108.42	247.06	545.76
22	1.245	1.546	1.916	2.370	2.925	3.603	4.430	5.436	6.658	8.140	9.933	12.100	14.713	17.861	21.644	26.186	55.205	135.53	321.18	736.78
23	1.257	1.577	1.974	2.465	3.071	3.820	4.740	5.871	7.258	8.954	11.026	13.552	16.626	20.361	24.891	30.376	66.247	169.41	417.53	994.65
24	1.270	1.608	2.033	2.563	3.225	4.049	5.072	6.341	7.911	9.850	12.239	15.178	18.788	23.212	28.625	35.236	79.496	211.76	542.79	1342.8
25	1.282	1.641	2.094	2.666	3.386	4.292	5.427	6.848	8.623	10.834	13.585	17.000	21.230	26.461	32.918	40.874	95.395	264.70	705.63	1812.8
30	1.348	1.811	2.427	3.243	4.322	5.743	7.612	10.062	13.267	17.449	22.892	29.960	39.115	50.949	66.210	85.849	237.37	807.79	2619.9	8128.4
35	1.417	2.000	2.814	3.946	5.516	7.686	10.676	14.785	20.413	28.102	38.574	52.799	72.066	98.097	133.17	180.31	590.66	2465.2	9727.6	36448.
40	1.489	2.208	3.262	4.801	7.040	10.285	14.974	21.724	31.408	45.258	64.999	93.049	132.78	188.88	267.86	378.72	1469.7	7523.2	36118.	*
45	1.565	2.438	3.781	5.841	8.985	13.764	21.002	31.920	48.325	72.888	109.53	163.99	244.63	363.66	538.75	795.43	3657.2	22959.	*	*
50	1.645	2.691	4.384	7.106	11.467	18.419	29.456	46.900	74.354	117.39	184.56	289.00	450.71	700.20	1083.6	1670.7	9100.2	70065.	*	*

*FVIF > 99.999

36

TABLE 2 — Future-Value Interest Factors for a One Dollar Annuity Compounded at *k* Percent for *n* Periods: $FVIFA_{k,n} = \sum_{t=1}^{N} (1+k)^{t-1}$

Period	1%	2%	3%	4%	5%	6%	7%	8%	9%	10%	11%	12%	13%	14%	15%	16%	20%	25%	30%	35%
1	1.000	1.000	1.000	1.000	1.000	1.000	1.000	1.000	1.000	1.000	1.000	1.000	1.000	1.000	1.000	1.000	1.000	1.000	1.000	1.000
2	2.010	2.020	2.030	2.040	2.050	2.060	2.070	2.080	2.090	2.100	2.110	2.120	2.130	2.140	2.150	2.160	2.200	2.250	2.300	2.350
3	3.030	3.060	3.091	3.122	3.152	3.184	3.215	3.246	3.278	3.310	3.342	3.374	3.407	3.440	3.472	3.506	3.640	3.813	3.990	4.172
4	4.060	4.122	4.184	4.246	4.310	4.375	4.440	4.506	4.573	4.641	4.710	4.779	4.850	4.921	4.993	5.066	5.368	5.766	6.187	6.633
5	5.101	5.204	5.309	5.416	5.526	5.637	5.751	5.867	5.985	6.105	6.228	6.353	6.480	6.610	6.742	6.877	7.442	8.207	9.043	9.954
6	6.152	6.308	6.468	6.633	6.802	6.975	7.153	7.336	7.523	7.716	7.913	8.115	8.323	8.535	8.754	8.977	9.930	11.259	12.756	14.438
7	7.214	7.434	7.662	7.898	8.142	8.394	8.654	8.923	9.200	9.487	9.783	10.089	10.405	10.730	11.067	11.414	12.916	15.073	17.583	20.492
8	8.286	8.583	8.892	9.214	9.549	9.897	10.260	10.637	11.028	11.436	11.859	12.300	12.757	13.233	13.727	14.240	16.499	19.842	23.858	28.664
9	9.368	9.755	10.159	10.583	11.027	11.491	11.978	12.488	13.021	13.579	14.164	14.776	15.416	16.085	16.786	17.518	20.799	25.802	32.015	39.696
10	10.462	10.950	11.464	12.006	12.578	13.181	13.816	14.487	15.193	15.937	16.722	17.549	18.420	19.337	20.304	21.321	25.959	33.253	42.619	54.590
11	11.567	12.169	12.808	13.486	14.207	14.972	15.784	16.645	17.560	18.531	19.561	20.655	21.814	23.044	24.349	25.733	32.150	42.566	56.405	74.696
12	12.682	13.412	14.192	15.026	15.917	16.870	17.888	18.977	20.141	21.384	22.713	24.133	25.650	27.271	29.001	30.850	39.580	54.208	74.326	101.84
13	13.809	14.680	15.618	16.627	17.713	18.882	20.141	21.495	22.953	24.523	26.211	28.029	29.984	32.088	34.352	36.786	48.496	68.760	97.624	138.48
14	14.947	15.974	17.086	18.292	19.598	21.015	22.550	24.215	26.019	27.975	30.095	32.392	34.882	37.581	40.504	43.672	59.196	86.949	127.91	187.95
15	16.097	17.293	18.599	20.023	21.578	23.276	25.129	27.152	29.361	31.772	34.405	37.280	40.417	43.842	47.580	51.659	72.035	109.69	167.29	254.74
16	17.258	18.639	20.157	21.824	23.657	25.672	27.888	30.324	33.003	35.949	39.190	42.753	46.671	50.980	55.717	60.925	87.442	138.11	218.47	344.90
17	18.430	20.012	21.761	23.697	25.840	28.213	30.840	33.750	36.973	40.544	44.500	48.883	53.738	59.117	65.075	71.673	105.93	173.64	285.01	466.61
18	19.614	21.412	23.414	25.645	28.132	30.905	33.999	37.450	41.301	45.599	50.396	55.749	61.724	68.393	75.836	84.140	128.12	218.05	371.51	630.92
19	20.811	22.840	25.117	27.671	30.539	33.760	37.379	41.446	46.018	51.158	56.939	63.439	70.748	78.968	88.211	98.603	154.74	273.56	483.97	852.74
20	22.019	24.297	26.870	29.778	33.066	36.785	40.995	45.762	51.159	57.274	64.202	72.052	80.946	91.024	102.44	115.38	186.69	342.95	630.16	1152.2
21	23.239	25.783	28.676	31.969	35.719	39.992	44.865	50.422	56.764	64.002	72.264	81.698	92.468	104.77	118.81	134.84	225.02	429.68	820.20	1556.5
22	24.471	27.299	30.536	34.248	38.505	43.392	49.005	55.456	62.872	71.402	81.213	92.502	105.49	120.43	137.63	157.41	271.03	538.10	1067.3	2102.2
23	25.716	28.845	32.452	36.618	41.430	46.995	53.435	60.893	69.531	79.542	91.147	104.60	120.20	138.30	159.27	183.60	326.23	673.63	1388.4	2839.0
24	26.973	30.421	34.426	39.082	44.501	50.815	58.176	66.764	76.789	88.496	102.17	118.15	136.83	158.66	184.17	213.98	392.48	843.03	1806.0	3833.7
25	28.243	32.030	36.459	41.645	47.726	54.864	63.248	73.105	84.699	98.346	114.41	133.33	155.62	181.87	212.79	249.21	471.98	1054.8	2348.8	5176.4
30	34.784	40.567	47.575	56.084	66.438	79.057	94.459	113.28	136.31	164.49	199.02	241.33	293.19	356.78	434.74	530.31	1181.9	3227.2	8729.8	23221.
35	41.659	49.994	60.461	73.651	90.318	111.43	138.23	172.31	215.71	271.02	341.58	431.66	546.66	693.55	881.15	1120.7	2948.3	9856.7	32422.	*
40	48.885	60.401	75.400	95.024	120.80	154.76	199.63	259.05	337.87	442.58	581.81	767.08	1013.7	1342.0	1779.0	2360.7	7343.7	30089.	*	*
45	56.479	71.891	92.718	121.03	159.70	212.74	285.74	386.50	525.84	718.88	986.61	1358.2	1874.1	2590.5	3585.0	4965.2	18281.	91831.	*	*
50	64.461	84.577	112.79	152.66	209.34	290.33	406.52	573.76	815.05	1163.9	1668.7	2400.0	3459.3	4994.3	7217.5	10435.	45496.	*	*	*

*FVIFA > 99,999.

37

TABLE 3 — Present-Value Interest Factors for One Dollar Discounted at k Percent for n Periods: $PVIF_{k,n} = 1/(1 + k)^n$

Period	1%	2%	3%	4%	5%	6%	7%	8%	9%	10%	11%	12%	13%	14%	15%	16%	17%	18%	19%	20%	25%	30%	35%
1	.990	.980	.971	.962	.952	.943	.935	.926	.917	.909	.901	.893	.885	.877	.870	.862	.855	.847	.840	.833	.800	.769	.741
2	.980	.961	.943	.925	.907	.890	.873	.857	.842	.826	.812	.797	.783	.769	.756	.743	.731	.718	.706	.694	.640	.592	.549
3	.971	.942	.915	.889	.864	.840	.816	.794	.772	.751	.731	.712	.693	.675	.658	.641	.624	.609	.593	.579	.512	.455	.406
4	.961	.924	.888	.855	.823	.792	.763	.735	.708	.683	.659	.636	.613	.592	.572	.552	.534	.516	.499	.482	.410	.350	.301
5	.951	.906	.863	.822	.784	.747	.713	.681	.650	.621	.593	.567	.543	.519	.497	.476	.456	.437	.419	.402	.328	.269	.223
6	.942	.888	.837	.790	.746	.705	.666	.630	.596	.564	.535	.507	.480	.456	.432	.410	.390	.370	.352	.335	.262	.207	.165
7	.933	.871	.813	.760	.711	.665	.623	.583	.547	.513	.482	.452	.425	.400	.376	.354	.333	.314	.296	.279	.210	.159	.122
8	.923	.853	.789	.731	.677	.627	.582	.540	.502	.467	.434	.404	.376	.351	.327	.305	.285	.266	.249	.233	.168	.123	.091
9	.914	.837	.766	.703	.645	.592	.544	.500	.460	.424	.391	.361	.333	.308	.284	.263	.243	.225	.209	.194	.134	.094	.067
10	.905	.820	.744	.676	.614	.558	.508	.463	.422	.386	.352	.322	.295	.270	.247	.227	.208	.191	.176	.162	.107	.073	.050
11	.896	.804	.722	.650	.585	.527	.475	.429	.388	.350	.317	.287	.261	.237	.215	.195	.178	.162	.148	.135	.086	.056	.037
12	.887	.789	.701	.625	.557	.497	.444	.397	.356	.319	.286	.257	.231	.208	.187	.168	.152	.137	.124	.112	.069	.043	.027
13	.879	.773	.681	.601	.530	.469	.415	.368	.326	.290	.258	.229	.204	.182	.163	.145	.130	.116	.104	.093	.055	.033	.020
14	.870	.758	.661	.577	.505	.442	.388	.340	.299	.263	.232	.205	.181	.160	.141	.125	.111	.099	.088	.078	.044	.025	.015
15	.861	.743	.642	.555	.481	.417	.362	.315	.275	.239	.209	.183	.160	.140	.123	.108	.095	.084	.074	.065	.035	.020	.011
16	.853	.728	.623	.534	.458	.394	.339	.292	.252	.218	.188	.163	.141	.123	.107	.093	.081	.071	.062	.054	.028	.015	.008
17	.844	.714	.605	.513	.436	.371	.317	.270	.231	.198	.170	.146	.125	.108	.093	.080	.069	.060	.052	.045	.023	.012	.006
18	.836	.700	.587	.494	.416	.350	.296	.250	.212	.180	.153	.130	.111	.095	.081	.069	.059	.051	.044	.038	.018	.009	.005
19	.828	.686	.570	.475	.396	.331	.277	.232	.194	.164	.138	.116	.098	.083	.070	.060	.051	.043	.037	.031	.014	.007	.003
20	.820	.673	.554	.456	.377	.312	.258	.215	.178	.149	.124	.104	.087	.073	.061	.051	.043	.037	.031	.026	.012	.005	.002
21	.811	.660	.538	.439	.359	.294	.242	.199	.164	.135	.112	.093	.077	.064	.053	.044	.037	.031	.026	.022	.009	.004	.002
22	.803	.647	.522	.422	.342	.278	.226	.184	.150	.123	.101	.083	.068	.056	.046	.038	.032	.026	.022	.018	.007	.003	.001
23	.795	.634	.507	.406	.326	.262	.211	.170	.138	.112	.091	.074	.060	.049	.040	.033	.027	.022	.018	.015	.006	.002	.001
24	.788	.622	.492	.390	.310	.247	.197	.158	.126	.102	.082	.066	.053	.043	.035	.028	.023	.019	.015	.013	.005	.002	.001
25	.780	.610	.478	.375	.295	.233	.184	.146	.116	.092	.074	.059	.047	.038	.030	.024	.020	.016	.013	.010	.004	.001	.001
30	.742	.552	.412	.308	.231	.174	.131	.099	.075	.057	.044	.033	.026	.020	.015	.012	.009	.007	.005	.004	.001	*	*
35	.706	.500	.355	.253	.181	.130	.094	.068	.049	.036	.026	.019	.014	.010	.008	.006	.004	.003	.002	.002	*	*	*
40	.672	.453	.307	.208	.142	.097	.067	.046	.032	.022	.015	.011	.008	.005	.004	.003	.002	.001	.001	.001	*	*	*
45	.639	.410	.264	.171	.111	.073	.048	.031	.021	.014	.009	.006	.004	.003	.002	.001	.001	.001	*	*	*	*	*
50	.608	.372	.228	.141	.087	.054	.034	.021	.013	.009	.005	.003	.002	.001	.001	.001	*	*	*	*	*	*	*

*PVIF = .000 when rounded to three decimal places.

38

TABLE 4 — Future-Value Interest Factors for a One Dollar Annuity Discounted at *k* Percent for *n* Periods: $PVIFA_{k,n} = \sum\limits_{t=1}^{n} 1/(1+k)^t$

Period	1%	2%	3%	4%	5%	6%	7%	8%	9%	10%	11%	12%	13%	14%	15%	16%	17%	18%	19%	20%	25%	30%	35%
1	.990	.980	.971	.962	.952	.943	.935	.926	.917	.909	.901	.893	.885	.877	.870	.862	.855	.847	.840	.833	.800	.769	.741
2	1.970	1.942	1.913	1.886	1.859	1.833	1.808	1.783	1.759	1.736	1.713	1.690	1.668	1.647	1.626	1.605	1.585	1.566	1.547	1.528	1.440	1.361	1.289
3	2.941	2.884	2.829	2.775	2.723	2.673	2.624	2.577	2.531	2.487	2.444	2.402	2.361	2.322	2.283	2.246	2.210	2.174	2.140	2.106	1.952	1.816	1.696
4	3.902	3.808	3.717	3.630	3.546	3.465	3.387	3.312	3.240	3.170	3.102	3.037	2.974	2.914	2.855	2.798	2.743	2.690	2.639	2.589	2.362	2.166	1.997
5	4.853	4.713	4.580	4.452	4.329	4.212	4.100	3.993	3.890	3.791	3.696	3.605	3.517	3.433	3.352	3.274	3.199	3.127	3.058	2.991	2.689	2.436	2.220
6	5.795	5.601	5.417	5.242	5.076	4.917	4.767	4.623	4.486	4.355	4.231	4.111	3.998	3.889	3.784	3.685	3.589	3.498	3.410	3.326	2.951	2.643	2.385
7	6.728	6.472	6.230	6.002	5.786	5.582	5.389	5.206	5.033	4.868	4.712	4.564	4.423	4.288	4.160	4.039	3.922	3.812	3.706	3.605	3.161	2.802	2.508
8	7.652	7.326	7.020	6.733	6.463	6.210	5.971	5.747	5.535	5.335	5.146	4.968	4.799	4.639	4.487	4.344	4.207	4.078	3.954	3.837	3.329	2.925	2.598
9	8.566	8.162	7.786	7.435	7.108	6.802	6.515	6.247	5.995	5.759	5.537	5.328	5.132	4.946	4.772	4.607	4.451	4.303	4.163	4.031	3.463	3.019	2.665
10	9.471	8.983	8.530	8.111	7.722	7.360	7.024	6.710	6.418	6.145	5.889	5.650	5.426	5.216	5.019	4.833	4.659	4.494	4.339	4.192	3.570	3.092	2.715
11	10.368	9.787	9.253	8.760	8.306	7.887	7.499	7.139	6.805	6.495	6.207	5.938	5.687	5.453	5.234	5.029	4.836	4.656	4.486	4.327	3.656	3.147	2.752
12	11.255	10.575	9.954	9.385	8.863	8.384	7.943	7.536	7.161	6.814	6.492	6.194	5.918	5.660	5.421	5.197	4.988	4.793	4.611	4.439	3.725	3.190	2.779
13	12.134	11.348	10.635	9.986	9.394	8.853	8.358	7.904	7.487	7.013	6.750	6.424	6.122	5.842	5.583	5.342	5.118	4.910	4.715	4.533	3.780	3.223	2.799
14	13.004	12.106	11.296	10.563	9.899	9.295	8.745	8.244	7.786	7.367	6.982	6.628	6.302	6.002	5.724	5.468	5.229	5.008	4.802	4.611	3.824	3.249	2.814
15	13.865	12.849	11.938	11.118	10.380	9.712	9.108	8.560	8.061	7.606	7.191	6.811	6.462	6.142	5.847	5.575	5.324	5.092	4.876	4.675	3.859	3.268	2.825
16	14.718	13.578	12.561	11.652	10.838	10.106	9.447	8.851	8.313	7.824	7.379	6.974	6.604	6.265	5.954	5.668	5.405	5.162	4.938	4.730	3.887	3.283	2.834
17	15.562	14.292	13.166	12.166	11.274	10.477	9.763	9.122	8.544	8.022	7.549	7.120	6.729	6.373	6.047	5.749	5.475	5.222	4.990	4.775	3.910	3.295	2.840
18	16.398	14.992	13.754	12.659	11.690	10.828	10.059	9.372	8.756	8.201	7.702	7.250	6.840	6.467	6.128	5.818	5.534	5.273	5.033	4.812	3.928	3.304	2.844
19	17.226	15.679	14.374	13.134	12.085	11.158	10.336	9.604	8.950	8.365	7.839	7.366	6.938	6.550	6.198	5.877	5.584	5.316	5.070	4.843	3.942	3.311	2.848
20	18.046	16.352	14.878	13.590	12.462	11.470	10.594	9.818	9.129	8.514	7.963	7.469	7.025	6.623	6.259	5.929	5.628	5.353	5.101	4.870	3.954	3.316	2.850
21	18.857	17.011	15.415	14.029	12.821	11.764	10.836	10.017	9.292	8.649	8.075	7.562	7.102	6.687	6.312	5.973	5.665	5.384	5.127	4.891	3.963	3.320	2.852
22	19.661	17.658	15.937	14.451	13.163	12.042	11.061	10.201	9.442	8.772	8.176	7.645	7.170	6.743	6.359	6.011	5.696	5.410	5.149	4.909	3.970	3.323	2.853
23	20.456	18.292	16.444	14.857	13.489	12.303	11.272	10.371	9.580	8.883	8.266	7.718	7.230	6.792	6.399	6.044	5.723	5.432	5.167	4.925	3.976	3.325	2.854
24	21.244	18.914	16.936	15.247	13.799	12.550	11.469	10.529	9.707	8.985	8.348	7.784	7.283	6.835	6.434	6.073	5.746	5.451	5.182	4.937	3.981	3.327	2.855
25	22.023	19.524	17.413	15.622	14.094	12.783	11.654	10.675	9.823	9.077	8.422	7.843	7.330	6.873	6.464	6.097	5.766	5.467	5.195	4.948	3.985	3.329	2.856
30	25.808	22.396	19.601	17.292	15.373	13.765	12.409	11.258	10.274	9.427	8.694	8.055	7.496	7.003	6.566	6.177	5.829	5.517	5.235	4.979	3.995	3.332	2.857
35	29.409	24.999	21.487	18.665	16.374	14.498	12.948	11.655	10.567	9.644	8.855	8.176	7.586	7.070	6.617	6.215	5.858	5.539	5.251	4.992	3.998	3.333	2.857
40	32.835	27.356	23.115	19.793	17.159	15.046	13.332	11.925	10.757	9.779	8.951	8.244	7.634	7.105	6.642	6.233	5.871	5.548	5.258	4.997	3.999	3.333	2.857
45	36.095	29.490	24.519	20.720	17.774	15.456	13.606	12.108	10.881	9.863	9.008	8.283	7.661	7.123	6.654	6.242	5.877	5.552	5.261	4.999	4.000	3.333	2.857
50	39.196	31.424	25.730	21.482	18.256	15.762	13.801	12.233	10.962	9.915	9.042	8.304	7.675	7.133	6.661	6.246	5.880	5.554	5.262	4.999	4.000	3.333	2.857

39

CHAPTER 8

RISK AND RETURN

8.1 RISK AND RETURN

Risk is defined as the variability of returns associated with a particular asset.

Return is defined as the total gain or loss experienced by the owner of an asset over a given time period. For a common stock, the rate of return (k) formula would be:

$$k_t = \frac{P_t - P_{t-1} + D}{P_{t-1}}$$

where P_t = price of stock this period
          P_{t-1} = price of stock last period
          D = dividend

A risk-averse investor does not like risk and must be given increasing returns as a condition of accepting additional risk.

A risk-indifferent investor is willing to accept increasing levels of risk without an increase in return.

A risk-taker or risk-seeker investor enjoys risk and is willing to accept lower returns as the level of risk increases.

Financial theory assumes that investors are risk averse and require compensation for assuming additional risk.

8.2 MEASURING RISK – SINGLE ASSET

The most common methods for measuring risk of a single asset involves the use of probability. Probability is the likelihood of occurrence for an event.

Probabilities may be used to quantify a **three-level estimate**. A three-level estimate typically involves making a pessimistic estimate, optimistic estimate and a "most likely" estimate. Probabilities, totalling 1.0, may be attached to each estimate.

A continuous probability distribution may be used. The most common form of the continuous probability distribution is the "normal" or "bell shaped" distribution.

The wider the dispersion of the distribution, the greater the risk. **Standard deviation** is one method measuring this dispersion. Standard deviation is an **absolute** measure of deviation from an expected value.

If the returns from two assets have different expected values, a measure of **relative** dispersion is needed. The **coefficient of variation** is the measure commonly calculated to compare distributions involving different expected values.

Sensitivity analysis is a common method for analyzing risk. Three-level estimates are one form of sensitivity analysis. Sensitivity analysis involves changing different variables to test the sensitivity of the outcome to its variables.

Computer simulation assigns a probability distribution to each variable then, using the random number generator of the computer, calculates the result with a large number of trials. An expected value and standard deviation is then calculated for these trials.

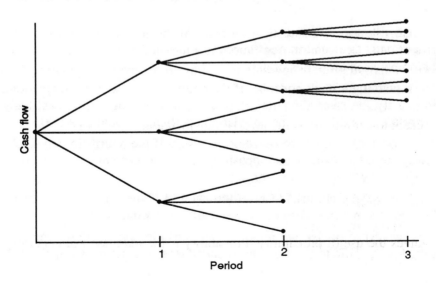

41

A **probability tree** is another method for analyzing the risk in a project. With a probability tree, possible outcomes are estimated by time period, based upon the events of the previous time period. A probability tree is illustrated above.

Estimates of cash flow and probabilities for each estimate (**initial probabilities**) are made for period 1. Period 2 contains estimated cash flows based upon period 1 cash flows, with probability estimates (**conditional probabilities**). Period 3 is estimated in a similiar manner. Each outcome at the end of period 3 has a **joint probability**, which is the product of the initial probability and the conditional probabilities of periods 2 and 3. The joint probability times the cash flow for each branch is summed to give a weighted average or expected value return.

8.3 MEASURING RISK - PORTFOLIO

A **portfolio** is two or more assets. These assets can be financial assets, such as stocks and bonds, or physical assets.

The **expected return from a portfolio** is equal to the weighted average of the expected return of the individual investments in the portfolio.

The **riskiness** of expected return from a portfolio cannot be measured by the weighted average of the individual standard deviations. Correlation of the expected returns is important in assessing risk of a portfolio.

Correlation is a statistical measure of the relationship between series of data. **Correlation coefficient** is a measure of the degree of correlation between the series of data.

Assuming a stock portfolio, if the returns of two stocks always move in exactly the same direction, they are said to be **perfectly positively correlated**. In this case, the correlation coefficient would be +1.00.

A **perfectly negative correlation** results if the returns to two stocks always move in exactly the opposite direction to each other. This would be shown by a correlation coefficient of −1.00.

Two stocks are said to be **uncorrelated** if there is no relationship between the returns. The correlation coefficient would be 0.

Two types of risk are important in portfolio construction. One type of risk is specific to the firm and is called **unsystematic risk** or **diversi-**

fiable risk. Risk specific to the firm can be diversified away in portfolio construction and investors are not compensated for this risk.

Systematic risk or **non-diversifiable risk** is the risk of the entire market and cannot be diversified away. Systematic risk is the only relevant risk. Market risk is used interchangeably with systematic risk.

An **efficient portfolio** maximizes the return for a given level of risk or minimizes risk for a given level of return.

The **market portfolio** consists of all available investments, including financial and real assets. There is not a measure of the market portfolio; however, the *Standard & Poor's 500 Index*, the *New York Stock Exchange Index* or the *Wilshire 5000 Index* are normally used as a proxy for the market portfolio in the Capital Asset Pricing Model.

The **Capital Asset Pricing Model** (CAPM) is the basic theory that relates risk and return for all assets. The formula is shown below:

$$R_j = R_F + \beta \, (R_M - R_F)$$

where: R_j = required return on security j,
R_F = risk-free rate
b = beta for the stock
R_M = return on the market
$R_M - R_F$ = market risk

The beta coefficient β is a relative risk measure and is equal to the covariance of returns between the security and the market divided by the variance of the market returns. It is an index of the degree of movement of an asset's return in response to a change in the market return.

$$Beta_x = \frac{Cov_{x,M}}{Var_M} = \frac{r_{x,M}\sigma_x\sigma_m}{\sigma^2 m}$$

where: $r_{x,M}$ = correlation of returns between stock x and the market
σ_x = variability of returns of security x
σ_M = variability of returns of the market
σ_{2M} = variance of the market returns

Several important assumptions underlie the CAPM model:

1. Investors seek to maximize the utility of their wealth position.
2. CAPM assumes a single period investment horizon.

3. Investors are assumed to have homogeneous expectations.

4. Investors can borrow or lend at the risk-free rate.

5. Markets are assumed to be perfectly efficient — no transaction cost, no taxes, perfect divisibility and no investor large enough to affect the market.

The **Security Market Line** is a graphical representation of the relationship between the risk-free rate and market premium for risk.

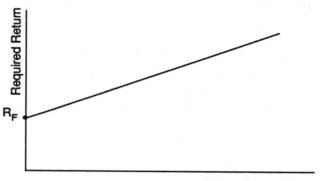

The Security Market Line (SML) graphically represents the risk/return tradeoff on security returns. The SML intersects the vertical axis at the risk free (R) interest rate and represents the current minimum required return. As risk increases, as measured by beta, the required rate of return increases. Increased returns can only be achieved by accepting increased risk.

The December 23, 1988 issue of *Value Line* reported the following betas:

Chrysler Corporation	1.45
General Motors Corporation	.95
Ford Motor Corporation	1.20

This indicated that General Motors has less systematic risk than Ford and Chrysler and thus the required return on the stock would be less. The market measure, such as the S & P 500 Index, has a beta of 1.0, thus GMC stock will not advance as rapidly as the Index or fall as rapidly as the Index. Ford and Chrysler are more volatile than the Index, hence, more risky.

CHAPTER 9

VALUATION

9.1   VALUATION FUNDAMENTALS

The basic valuation formula for all assets, whether financial or real assets, is the discounted value of all future cash flows. Thus, there are three key inputs to the valuation process: amount of the cash flow, timing of the cash flow, and the discount rate.

There are several definitions of value. However, all ultimately depend upon the basic valuation formula.

Liquidating value is the value which would result from selling the assets, individually or in groups, separate from the business organization. Liquidating value decreases as the time allowed for selling the asset decreases.

Going concern value is the value which would result from selling the entire business, including assets, as an operating business complete with customers and a trained workforce.

Book value is the value of the assets or the firm as reflected in the financial statements. Book values represent accounting values based upon historical cost. Book value per share is calculated by adding all common equity accounts, such as common stock, paid in excess of par and returned earnings, and dividing by the number of common shares.

Market value is the value resulting from sale of the asset. Market values for financial assets, such as stocks and bonds, are reported regularly in the newspapers.

Intrinsic value is a term applied to financial assets and is the discounted cash flow value as calculated by an analyst after careful study of the firm and its industry.

45

9.2   VALUATION OF FIXED INCOME SECURITIES

The basic formula for valuing a bond is:

$$P_b = \sum_{t=1}^{n} \frac{I_t}{(1+k)^t} + \frac{P_n}{(1+k)^n}$$

where
P_b = the price of the bond,
I = the interest payments over the life of the bond,
P_n = the price of the bond when sold or redeemed (usually assumed to be the face value) and
k = the market rate of discount (required rate of return) for comparable financial assets.

Most bonds pay interest semiannually rather than annually. If I (above) represents a semiannual interest payment, then the formula would be:

$$P_b = \sum_{t=1}^{n} \frac{I_t}{(1+\frac{k}{2})^t} + \frac{P_n}{(1+\frac{k}{2})}$$

Yield to maturity is more difficult to calculate without a financial calculator. Yield to maturity (YTM) is the discount rate (k) that will make the future cash flows exactly equal the price. The process is called "internal rate of return" in capital budgeting. An approximate yield to maturity can be found using the following formula:

$$\text{Approximate YTM} = \frac{\text{Annual Interest Payment} + \dfrac{\text{Principal Payment} - \text{price of the bond}}{\text{number of years to maturity}}}{\dfrac{\text{Price of the bond} + \text{principal payment}}{2}}$$

As interest rates increase, prices of existing fixed income securities fall; as interest rates decline, prices of existing fixed income securities rise.

The longer the maturity of the fixed income security, the greater the changes in price resulting from interest rate changes.

Perpetual bonds never mature and have occasionally been issued by governments. The formula for a perpetual bond is:

$$P = \frac{I}{k}$$

where I = interest payment

Preferred stock, except participating preferred, are fixed income securities and are perpetuities. Thus, their valuation formula is similar to a perpetual bond

$$P = \frac{D}{k}$$

where D = dividend

9.3 VALUATION OF COMMON STOCK

The basic equation for valuing common stock is:

$$P_0 = \frac{D_1}{(1+k)^1} + \frac{D_2}{(1+k)^2} + ... + \frac{D_\infty}{(1+k)_\infty}$$

This formula states that today's price is equal to the sum of the discounted value of all future dividends, including the liquidating dividend. Sale of the stock is equivalent to a liquidating dividend.

As shown in the basic equation, valuation of common stock is usually treated as a perpetuity. Thus, if no growth in dividends is assumed, the formula is:

$$P_0 = \frac{D_1}{k}$$

which is the same as preferred stock.

9.3.1 CONSTANT GROWTH MODEL

The normal assumption for common stock is that dividends will grow over time. The expected return (k) on common stock is equal to the dividend yield plus the percentage growth rate of dividends over time (g). Thus:

$$\hat{k} = \frac{D}{P} + g$$

In valuing a common stock with a growing dividend stream, we define "k" as our desired return and the equation is written thus:

$$P_0 = \frac{D_1}{k - g}$$

9.3.2 VARIABLE GROWTH MODEL

A new firm may grow rapidly during its early years then slow to a more sustainable growth rate. In this situation, the dividends for the rapid growth period are valued and the value of the stock price at the end of this period is calculated. The formula would be as follows:

$$P_0 = \sum_{t=1}^{m} \frac{D_t}{(1+k)^t} + \frac{1}{(1+k)^n} \times \frac{D_{n+1}}{k-g}$$

<table>
<tr><td>Present value of dividends, rapid growth stage</td><td>Present value of price of stock at end of initial growth period</td></tr>
</table>

9.3.3 PRICE EARNINGS RATIO

The Price Earnings ratio (PE ratio) is widely used to estimate the value of stock. It is calculated by dividing Price by Earnings per Share and can be found in the financial pages of most newspapers or on the Web. It is a less sophisticated measure than the dividend models but is used by many investors and professionals. Industry average PE ratios are sometimes used to estimate the value of privately held corporations.

9.4 REQUIRED RATES OF RETURN

The required rate of return "k" can be calculated from the capital asset pricing model (CAPM) as illustrated below and explained under "Risk and Return." The risk free rate (R)

$$k = R_F + \beta(R_M - R_F)$$

changes as inflation rate expectations, economic conditions, international trade imbalances, etc., change. The market risk premium ($R - R_F$) changes as investors become "bullish" or "bearish." Beta (β) changes as investors perceive the cash flow for the firm as more or less risky compared to the market portfolio.

The market price of a stock is affected by expectations of a change in the dollar amount of dividend (D_1) plus the expected future growth in the dividend (g). In addition, the price of the stock is affected by changes

48

in the perceived risk (k) of the stock.

$$P = \frac{D}{k - g}$$

Frequently expected return ($\hat{k}$) and required return (k) are used interchangeably. They are the same under conditions of market equilibrium; however, they may not be the same in all cases. Expected rate of return is equal to dividend yield plus expected capital gains resulting from growth in dividends.

$$\hat{k} = \frac{D}{P} + g$$

Required rate of return is equal to the interest free rate plus a risk premium, as in the CAPM model.

CHAPTER 10

CAPITAL BUDGETING

10.1 THE CAPITAL BUDGETING PROCESS

The capital budgeting process involves long range and short range planning. The principal components are outlined below.

Long range capital planning is an important first step in the process. This involves developing the future strategy for growth and estimating its investment and financing requirements. The financing strategy needs to be developed.

Short range financial planning is completed concurrently with the preparation of the capital budget. This step involves preparation of a cash budget and pro forma income statements and balance sheets.

Project evaluation involves analysis of the project cash flows, an evaluation of the risk of the cash flows and an examination of strategic and other non-quantifiable factors in the decision.

Project selection involves using the data and other information developed in the project evaluation component, considering such special circumstances as capital rationing and mutually exclusive projects, and selecting the projects to be authorized.

Control of authorized expenditures is an important step in the implementation of the capital projects. As the project is under construction, actual costs should be regularly compared with budgeted costs. If the deviation of actual from budgeted exceeds some agreed standard, cost control should be reviewed and the continued feasibility of the project examined.

Post-Completion Audit is used for major projects and should be performed after all costs are known, the process "debugged" and employees have completed the learning curve. This component allows the adequacy of the capital budgeting process to be analyzed and corrective action taken for systematic errors.

10.2 RELEVANT CASH FLOWS

The only relevant cash flows are incremental cash flows — those cash flows which would not occur in the absence of a project. An incremental cash flow can be an increase or a decrease from the cash flows occurring in the absence of the project.

The typical major cash flows to be accounted for in a capital budgeting analysis consist of the initial investment, the operating cash flows and the terminal cash flow.

Project costs are not relevant to the analysis. Sunk costs are not incremental — they have already occurred and are unaffected by the decision. An example of a sunk cost is research and development which has resulted in a possible new product.

Opportunity costs must be considered as the opportunity foregone might have produced an incremental cash flow. For example, a building already owned could be used for the capital project being studied. If not used for the project, it might be sold or leased to another firm.

The initial investment consists of the cost of the new asset, plus freight-in, plus installation cost, minus the proceeds from sale of the old asset, plus or minus taxes on sale of the old asset and plus or minus the change in net working capital with and without the new asset.

The operating cash flows for a new investment consist of the after-tax cash outflows and after-tax cash inflows associated with the new investment. After-tax cash flows are the relevant data rather than reported profits. Depreciation is relevant to the extent of its tax savings or "tax shield."

The operating cash flows for a replacement decision is the difference (or incremental) in after-tax cash flows from the existing asset and the proposed new asset.

The terminal cash flow consists of the incremental proceeds of the sale of the new asset versus the sale of the old asset. The incremental proceeds consist of the selling price of the new asset less any costs, such as dismantling, born by the seller, plus or minus any taxes on the sale. In addition, the market value of the old asset at this terminal time adjusted for taxes and plus or minus the change in net working capital must be subtracted. Because the market value of the old machine at this terminal time is usually negligible, this is usually ignored.

10.3 PROJECT EVALUATION

Project evaluation consists of analyzing the relevant cash flows for profitability and risk. Risk will be discussed in a separate section below. The basic approaches discussed in texts will be presented below; however, many variations of these basic approaches are in use in industry.

Accounting rate of return, or simple rate of return, involves the use of accounting profits rather than cash flows and does not discount for flows over time. The most common form consists of:

$$\text{rate of return} = \frac{\text{average annual profit}}{\text{average investment}}$$

This method is no longer included in some textbooks but is still used by some firms. Because it uses accounting profit rather than cash flow and does not recognize the time value of money, the rate of return calculated is not comparable to the rate of return using discounted cash flow methods or cost of capital calculations.

Payback is an evaluation method in common use in industry. This technique calculates the number of years required for cash flow to recover the original investment. Time value of money and cash flows past the payback period are ignored. A variation of this method, **the discounted payback**, calculates the present value of the cash flow for each year in determining the payback period.

Net Present Value (NPV) is the sum of the net operating cash flows plus the terminal value, each discounted at a specific discount rate, minus the original investment. The formula is:

$$\text{NPV} = \sum_{t=1}^{n} \frac{CF_t}{(1+k)^t} - I$$

where: I = original investment

CF = net cash flows by time period, including terminal cash flow

52

k = discount rate

The discount rate, sometimes called a **hurdle rate,** is typically based upon the firm's estimated cost of capital.

Internal Rate of Return (IRR) is the discount rate which equates the sum of the net operating cash flows plus the terminal value with the original investment. Thus, the formula is:

$$\text{IRR} = \sum_{t=1}^{n} \frac{CF_t}{(1+\text{IRR})^t} - I = \$0$$

or

$$\text{IRR} = \sum_{t=1}^{n} \frac{CF_t}{(1+\text{IRR})^t} = I$$

Although the NPV and IRR formulas are similar, there are important differences. These will be discussed in Section 10.4.

Profitability Index (PI) is a variation of NPV used for ranking projects. The formula for PI is:

$$\text{PI} = \frac{\displaystyle\sum_{t=1}^{n} \frac{CF_t}{(1+k)^t}}{I}$$

The main use for PI is in ranking projects under situations of capital rationing. This formula is simply the PV, not NPV, divided by the investment. The use of PI avoids the problems of IRR for ranking, as discussed in Section 10.4 and 10.6.

10.4 COMPARISON OF NET PRESENT VALUE AND INTERNAL RATE OF RETURN

As shown above, the differences in NPV and IRR involve the interest rate used and the form of the answer. The result of the NPV calculation is an answer in dollars while the IRR calculation results in an answer expressed as a percent. Businesspersons tend to find a percentage answer easier to understand.

The differences in the discount rate used results in significant differences as shown below.

(1) The discount rate used makes the implicit assumption that this

rate is the reinvestment rate for excess funds and the cost of funds for financing negative outflows. This infers, under IRR, that two proposed machine purchases for the same firm would have different reinvestment rates of return and financing rates if their IRR differs.

(2) According to Descartes' Rule of Signs and using the IRR formula, each time the sign of the cash flows changes, an additional solving rate of return will solve the equation. Thus, if the sign of the cash flows changes three times, theoretically there will be three different discount rates that will solve the equation. These "unconventional" cash flows can occur in projects where additional investment is needed in later years to prolong the project's life.

(3) Assuming conventional cash flows, NPV and IRR will always give the same accept-reject answer. They may, however, give conflicting ranking of projects depending upon the timing and magnitude of intermediate cash flows. The reinvestment rate assumption is the underlying cause for the conflicting rankings. Ranking becomes a concern under conditions of capital rationing or mutually exclusive projects.

10.5 INCORPORATING RISK IN THE CAPITAL DECISION

Certainty equivalents adjust the numerator while **risk adjusted discount rates** adjust the denominator. Adjusting the numerator is theoretically more correct because adjusting the denominator makes the implicit assumption that the risk is a linear function of time.

Certainty equivalents are based on indifference curves in economics. The certainty equivalent is that adjustment which causes the decision maker to be indifferent between the risky cash flow at time "t" and a certain cash flow at time "t". There are many practical problems in its application.

The use of certainty equivalents in adjusting for risk is illustrated below:

$$P_j = \sum_{t=1}^{\infty} \frac{\alpha_t \overline{D}_t}{(1+i)}$$

where
α_t = certainty equivalent adjustment (some value less than 1.0)

$\overline{D}_t$ = expected dividend, amount is uncertain

i = risk free interest rate

54

assume D_t = $10 level in perpetuity

α_t = .75 and i = .07, then

$$\frac{\alpha_t \overline{D}_t}{i} = \$107.14$$

Risk adjusted discount rates (RADR) are in common use in business. RADR are a subjectively based adjustment, upward or downward, from the discount rate used for the "average" risk project. This adjustment may be based upon probability analysis, sensitivity analysis, simulation, decision trees, capital asset pricing model, or "gut feeling" (Chapter 8). A firm may establish **risk classes** for projects, with each class having a different RADR. Each project is then assigned to a risk class.

The use of RADR in adjusting for risk is illustrated below:

$$P_j = \sum_{t=1}^{\infty} \frac{\overline{D}_t}{(1+r)}$$

where r = risk adjusted interest rate

assume r = .10, then $\overline{D}/_r$ = $100.

10.6 CAPITAL RATIONING

Capital rationing exists when a firm does not have the financial or managerial resources to accept all good capital projects. Ranking of projects then becomes necessary. The two most common methods for ranking projects are Internal Rate of Return and Profitability Index.

Internal Rate of Return (IRR), though frequently used, introduces the reinvestment rate problem which may cause conflicting rankings with NPV.

Profitability Index (PI) enables projects to be ranked by productivity while still being consistent with NPV.

Whichever ranking approach is used, the goal should be to maximize NPV for the capital budget accepted. Firms using IRR frequently also calculate NPV so that NPV can be included in their final decision.

10.7 MUTUALLY EXCLUSIVE PROJECTS

Mutually exclusive projects occur when the adoption of one project eliminates the possibility of adopting the other project. The general rule on mutually exclusive projects is to adopt the project with the highest NPV. If the projects have unequal lives, however, the maximizing NPV rule must be modified. Two methods, Replacement Chains and Annualized Net Present Value, are in common use.

Replacement Chains. Assume two projects, one with a five-year life and one with a ten-year life. It is assumed that at the end of the five-year project, another five-year project can be purchased at the same cost and yielding the same returns. The two ten-year projects are now compared using NPV.

Annualized Net Present Value (ANPV) or **Equal Annual Annuity (EAA) Method.** The replacement chains method requires that the project be converted to equal lives but this is not always possible. ANPV converts each project into a common base and can be applied to all projects. Calculation of ANPV involves the following steps:

1. Calculate NPV for each project.

2. Select all projects with a positive NPV.

3. Divide the NPV of each selected project by the present value interest factor for an annuity (PVIFA) at the given interest rate and the project's life. The result is the ANPV (EAA).

4. Select the project with the highest ANPV (EAA).

56

CHAPTER 11

COST OF CAPITAL

11.1 OVERVIEW OF THE CONCEPT

The cost of capital is simple in concept but complex in application. The cost of capital is the rate of return that must be earned on a project in order to maintain the market value of the firm's stock. Alternatively, it is the rate of return required by suppliers of capital on projects of similar risk.

Financial managers are concerned with **marginal cost of capital** — how much would it cost to raise capital now. They are not concerned with historical cost of capital for decision making.

11.2 COST OF LONG-TERM DEBT

Cost of capital is usually calculated on an after-tax basis. The **cost of long-term debt** is usually calculated on a before-tax basis, then adjusted to an after-tax basis. The net proceeds of the issue is the appropriate measure in calculating cost.

There are three methods for estimating the marginal cost of long-term debt.

1. Yield quotations from the financial news can be used. Sources such as the *Wall Street Journal* and *Barron's* have data on a large number and variety of bonds. The yield data in the financial news is **current yield**, which relates the interest paid to the purchase price. This is not the same as yield to maturity.

2. Calculating **yield to maturity** can be done with a financial calculator. Yield to maturity (YTM) is essentially the same as IRR. This was discussed previously under Valuation (See Chapter 9).

3. A third method is to approximate the cost using the following formula:

$$k_d = \frac{I + \dfrac{\$1,000 - N_d}{n}}{\dfrac{N_d + \$1,000}{2}}$$

where:
K_d = cost of debt
I = annual interest in dollars – assume $100
N_d = net proceeds from sale of debt – assume $990
n = number of years to maturity – assume 10 years

then:

$$k_d = \frac{100 + \dfrac{1,000 - 990}{10}}{\dfrac{990 + 1,000}{2}} = \frac{101}{995} = 10.15\%$$

The after-tax cost of debt (k_i) is found by multiplying the net proceeds from the sale of debt by $(1 - T)$, where T equals the tax rate.

11.3 COST OF PREFERRED STOCK

The cost of preferred stock is usually calculated as a perpetuity, using the following formula:

$$k_p = \frac{D_p}{N_p}$$

where:
k_p = cost of preferred stock
D_p = preferred dividends
N_p = net proceeds from sale of stock

11.4 THE COST OF COMMON STOCK

The typical methods used for estimating cost of common equity for business firms are the constant growth valuation model and the capital asset pricing model (CAPM).

The **constant growth valuation model**, frequently called the Gordon Model, is calculated by:

$$k_l = \frac{D_1}{P_0} + g$$

where:
    k_l = cost of common equity
    D_1 = estimated dividend in year 1
    P_o = present price of the stock
    g = expected future growth in dividends

The CAPM is calculated by:

$$k_l = R_F + \beta(k_m - R_F)$$

where:
    k_l = cost of common equity
    R_F = risk free rate
    β = beta
    k_m = return on the market portfolio

Cost of equity for financial decision making in traditional business firms is relatively non-controversial as it does not need to be defended. In public utilities rate cases, a minor variation in cost of equity has a significant effect on utility rates paid by rate payers. The measurement of almost every variable in the formulas are debated by experts. Additional cost of equity measures used in public utility cases are the risk premium method and Arbitrage Pricing Theory (APT); however, these approaches are not discussed in basic texts.

If a new issue of common stock must be sold, the price (P) in the Gordon Model is frequently adjusted to reflect underpricing and flotation costs. The formula then becomes:

$$k_l = \frac{D_1}{N_n} + g$$

where: N_n = net proceeds

or

$$k_l = \frac{D_1}{Po \times (1 - f)} + g$$

where: f = flotation costs

A new issue of securities is priced slightly below the market to reflect dilution in EPS and to encourage the rapid sale of the securities.

Flotation costs include all of the legal, accounting and printing costs associated with the filing with the Securities Exchange Commission and the commission fee for the underwriter.

11.5 WEIGHTED AVERAGE COST OF CAPITAL (WACC)

The WACC is calculated using weights based upon capital structure. The preferred method for calculating weights of the components of the capital structure is to use the **target capital structure,** with each component weighted by **market weights** rather than **book value weights.** Target capital structure is used because the actual capital structure at any point in time departs from the desired (target) capital structure due to financing, dept repayment, etc. The firm will try to maintain capital structure around its target capital structure over time. Market weights are more desirable than book value weights because market weights more nearly represent current (or marginal) costs.

The weighted average cost of capital formula is:

$$k_0 = (W_I \times k_I) + (W_p \times k_p) + (W_I \times k_I)$$

where:

k_0 = overall cost of capital
W_I = weighting of cost of debt – assume 40%
k_I = cost of debt – assume 5%
W_p = weighting of cost of preferred stock – assume 10%
k_p = cost of preferred stock – assume 9%
W_e = weighting of cost of equity (common stock) – assume 50%
k_e = cost of common equity — assume 15%

then:

$$k_0 = (.40 \times .05) + (.10 \times .09) + (.50 \times .15) = 10.4\%$$

Thus WACC as calculated is used as the basis for the denominator in discounting cash flows for capital budgeting purposes.

CHAPTER 12

CAPITAL STRUCTURE

12.1 OVERVIEW OF CAPITAL STRUCTURE

Capital structure consists of long-term debt, preferred stock and common equity. Financial structure consists of all liabilities, preferred equity and common equity.

Capital structure raises agency problems. Just as managers are agents for stockholders, managers and stockholders are agents for the suppliers of credit. Financial leverage gives owners and managers incentive to increase debt in the capital structure. Restrictions are imposed by long term creditors to ensure that capital structure remains acceptable to the creditors. Both creditors and investors use ratios to analyze the suitability of a firm's capital structure.

12.2 OPTIMAL CAPITAL STRUCTURE

The optimal capital structure is that combination of debt and equity that maximizes the market value of the firm's shares.

The traditional view of the optimal capital structure is shown graphically below.

Cost of debt and cost of equity each rise as financial leverage increases; however, WACC falls with early additions of debt because of the averaging of high-cost equity and low-cost debt. The Marginal Cost of Capital (MCC) crosses the WACC curve at its lowest point and WACC starts to rise. The intersection of the WACC curve and MCC curve is the optimal capital structure.

Contrary to the theoretical drawing above, it is believed that the WACC curve is comparatively flat over a reasonable range of capital

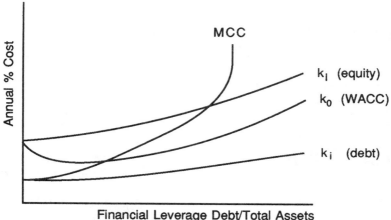

Financial Leverage Debt/Total Assets

structures. This allows some variation in structure without significantly increasing WACC.

12.3 RISK AND CAPITAL STRUCTURE

In general, the higher the operating leverage, the higher the business risk. Two other factors, however, influence business risk in addition to operating leverage.

These two factors are revenue stability and cost stability. Public utilities are capital intensive and thus have high operating leverage. The revenue stability and cost stability enjoyed by most public utilities, however, result in comparatively low business risk. The low business risk faced by most utilities enable them to use greater financial leverage without incurring excessive overall leverage.

A firm with high business risk will normally reduce the financial risk in their capital structure. Cost of debt and cost of equity will reflect investors' estimate of the combined business and financial risk.

12.4 CONSIDERATIONS IN CAPITAL STRUCTURE

There are several considerations in selecting a capital structure.

One such consideration is suitability. Is the financing need temporary or long-term? Temporary needs (seasonal) should be financed with temporary funds. Permanent needs are financed with permanent (long-term) funds.

One must also consider income when selecting a capital structure. What is the income advantage of financing with debt instead of equity? Is the financial leverage gained significant? Is the risk-return trade-off worth the additional risk? As shown earlier under the discussion of financial leverage, financing with debt when the degree of financial leverage (DOL) is significant can greatly increase earnings per share.

Another consideration factor is risk. How much additional risk is incurred by debt financing? Will forecasted cash flow adequately service the additional debt? Are revenues stable or unpredictable? What are management's views toward risks? How will investors and creditors view the increased risk if debt is used? As shown previously, income can increase significantly with the use of debt, assuming there is positive leverage; however, risk will also increase with additional debt. Whether the increased income compensates for the increased risk is a question the manager must decide.

Control is also a factor in selecting a capital structure. What are the principal owners' view of control of stockholders' voting? In a small firm, this consideration may be very important. In a large firm with wide public ownership, it may not be an issue.

Maneuverability should also be considered. How will the use of increased debt affect your ability to bargain and select funding sources in the future? What restrictions on future management decisions will be written into the proposed long-term debt contract? Today's financial decisions will affect tomorrow's operating and financial decisions. Positive and negative covenants in intermediate and long-term debt agreements require certain actions and prohibit others. The affects of today's financing on tomorrow's actions need to be analyzed as part of financial planning.

Yet another consideration in the selection of a capital structure is timing. What are the conditions in the capital markets? Is this a particularly opportune time to sell equity? Are bond interest rates particularly favorable at this time? Assuming that the WACC curve (and thus optimal capital structure) is flat over a significant range (saucer shaped), the firm may change capital structure partially in response to timing.

CHAPTER 13

CASH AND MARKETABLE SECURITIES

13.1 THE FUNCTION OF CASH MANAGEMENT

There are four primary reasons for firms to hold cash. They are:

1. Transactions motive — to pay bills when due.

2. Precautionary motive — to handle differences in timing of cash inflows and outflows.

3. Speculative motive — to enable a firm to take advantage of profitable opportunities on short notice.

4. Compensating balance requirements — minimum bank balances held in banks as partial compensation for services.

Cash management involves (1) managing the liquid funds of the firm in such a way that money is available to pay bills when due and (2) maximizing interest income, subject to risk constraints, on these liquid funds.

The treasurer usually has responsibility for cash management. The cash budget and daily cash reports are primary tools.

13.2 CASH MANAGEMENT TECHNIQUES

Cash management techniques mainly involve accelerating collections and controlling disbursements.

13.2.1 ACCELERATING COLLECTIONS

Float is the period of time that elapses from the time a check is written until the check clears the payer's bank account. Float operates on both collection and disbursing activities.

There are three kinds of float:

Mail time float — The amount of time which elapses between the customer mailing the check and the seller receiving the check.

Processing float — The amount of time which elapses between the seller receiving the check and its deposit into the seller's bank.

Transit float — The amount of time which elapses between the deposit of the check by the seller and its clearing by the payer's bank.

Accelerating collections involves developing techniques for reducing float.

Lockbox systems eliminate processing float, reduce mail float and may reduce transit float. A national firm establishes regional lockboxes, thus reducing mail time float. The lockbox (a mailbox) is cleared several times a day by the bank, which deposits the checks and sends customer payment information to the seller, thus eliminating processing float. Because the lockbox banks are closer to the customer, the transit float may be reduced.

Concentration banking involves moving all excess funds from depository banks to regional or a primary bank. Funds are then available for disbursement or short-term investments.

The main transfer mechanisms for transferring funds from one bank to another are as follows:

Depository transfer checks are ordinary checks which are restricted for deposit into a particular account at a particular bank.

Electronic Depository Transfer Checks use the electronic image transfer via the automated clearinghouses operated by the Federal Reserve System. The EDTC avoids the use of the mail and involves a one-day availability in clearing time.

Wire Transfer makes funds immediately available at another bank. It may utilize the private wire service operated by about 300 banks or the Federal Reserve System wire service.

Some banks offer a service that allows high-dollar-volume checks to be deposited directly into the drawee bank, thus eliminating transit float.

Electronic Funds Transfer systems involve the movement of funds between computer terminals without the use of a check. Customers pay for purchases at major retailers with cards which transfer the funds from their account at the time of purchase. Major firms have **treasury work**

consisting of computer terminals which monitor their bank accounts around the nation and transfer excess funds to a primary bank for disbursement or investment. Major banks also provide this service for corporate customers.

Automated Clearinghouses (ACHs) are important in EFT. An ACH transfers information between financial institutions via computer tape. **CHIPS**, the Clearing House Interbank System of New York banks, and **NACHA,** the National Automated Clearing House Association, are two of the ACH systems.

Multinational corporations use EFT to move funds from one country to another. One system for international funds transfer is known as **SWIFT**, the Society of Worldwide Interbanks Financial Telecommunications.

13.2.2 CONTROL OF DISBURSEMENTS

The objective of effective cash management is to accelerate the receipt of funds as much as possible while slowing disbursements as much as possible. Thus, if a supplier offers discounts for early payment, it should be paid on the last day that you will still receive the discount.

Under receipts, the cash manager attempts to minimize float; under disbursements, one attempts to maximize float. Among the approaches used to maximize float are the following:

Remote disbursement is the approach by which payables are paid by checks drawn on distant banks, especially banks in cities away from Federal Reserve Banks.

Bank drafts are sometimes used instead of checks as clearing is slower. When the draft arrives at the bank, the firm is notified and has until 3:00 PM to deposit the funds.

Some firms consider the discount date or due date to be met when the remittance is postmarked. Other firms require that the remittance be received by the discount date to qualify for the discount. Knowledge of your suppliers' practice enables you to time payments more closely.

The **zero balance account** is a device to minimize cash needs. An arrangement is made with the bank that the disbursement account will be kept at zero. Funds will be transferred in as needed to cover checks; the remaining funds are invested in short-term financial instruments.

Electronic Funds Transfer is also a tool in controlling cash disbursements. Payables can be paid by EFT on exactly the day desired.

13.3 MARKETABLE SECURITIES FUNDAMENTALS

Firms establish certain criteria to govern the operation of their marketable securities portfolio. These criteria are default risk, liquidity ability, interest rate risk, taxability, and relative yield.

Default risk — Most firms feel that they are in the business of producing a good or service, not investing, and thus safety of principal is usually an overriding criteria.

Liquidity ability — Liquidity is concerned with both the depth and breadth of the market. A wide variety of issues and maturities are desired and the market should have enough depth to absorb a significant sale of a security with minimal impact on price.

Interest Rate Risk — The longer the maturity of a debt instrument, the greater is the effect on price of an interest rate change. Firms, therefore, typically prefer short-term debt instruments.

Taxability — This is a significant issue for some firms, not for others. Tax advantage investments are not found in most marketable securities portfolios, probably because of liquidity and perceived risk concerns.

Relative yield — Within the risk and marketability constraints above, firms will try to maximize yield.

13.4 FINANCIAL INSTRUMENTS FOR A MARKETABLE SECURITIES PORTFOLIO

The following is a partial list of financial instruments used in a marketable securities portfolio.

Treasury securities include treasury bills, tax-anticipation bills, notes and bonds. As the notes and bonds approach maturity, they also serve the needs of short-term investors.

Agency securities — Many U.S. government agencies issue debt with a variety of maturities. They are guaranteed by the U.S. government and have a slightly higher yield.

Repurchase agreements (REPOS) are sale of government securities by government securities dealers and other financial institutions with an agreement to repurchase them at a specific date and specific price. Repos may be overnight or up to several weeks, depending upon the needs of the purchaser.

Commercial Paper — Short-term promissory notes by major corporations or by finance companies may be purchased from dealers or direct from finance companies. Major finance companies will tailor the maturity to the maturity needs of the buyer.

Negotiable Certificate of Deposit are large denomination CDs issued by money center banks that can be sold if the firm needs the funds. Firms also buy CDs of large foreign banks. These are called **Yankee CDs**.

Bankers Acceptances are drafts accepted by banks and used to finance foreign and domestic trade. Acceptances can also be on foreign banks. Acceptances are low risk depending upon the bank, and yields are comparable to commercial paper.

Eurodollars are dollar deposits in foreign banks or in foreign branches of U.S. Banks. Eurodollar deposits and financial instruments usually have a higher yield than U.S. marketable securities.

Adjustable-Rate Preferred Stock (ARPS) — Because the dividend income has a tax advantage to corporations, ARPS are used in some portfolios. ARPS is considered more risky because dividends are not a legal obligation.

13.5 CASH MANAGEMENT MODELS

The **Inventory Model** was first applied to cash management by William Baumol.

Assume C = cash balance
              T = total demand for cash over the time period involved
              b = fixed cost of the transaction
              i = interest rate on marketable securities

Thus:Total costs equal $b\left(\dfrac{T}{C}\right) + i\left(\dfrac{C}{2}\right)$

where $b\left(\dfrac{T}{C}\right)$ = fixed costs associated with transfers

$$i\left(\frac{C}{2}\right) = \text{opportunity cost of earnings foregone by holding cash balances.}$$

The objective is to minimize total cost.

The optimal level of C is found to be:

$$C^* = \sqrt{\frac{2bT}{i}}$$

Thus, cash demand will increase in relation to the square root of the dollar volume of cash payments.

The **Stockastic Model** (Control-Limits Model) was developed by Merton Miller and Daniel Orr and assumes cash demand is random. Two control limits are set — when the upper limit is reached, excess cash is invested in marketable securities; when the lower limit is reached, marketable securities are sold.

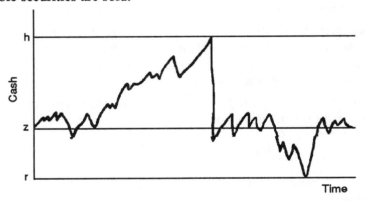

The optimum value for z, the return-to-point for securities transactions is:

$$z = \sqrt[3]{\frac{3b\sigma^2}{4i}}$$

where
b = fixed cost associated with a security transaction
σ^2 = variance of daily net cash flows
i = interest rate per day on marketable securities

The vertical axis represents cash balances. When cash balances reach some level (h), marketable securities equal to $h - z$ are purchased, returning the cash balances to z. When cash balances fall to some level (r), marketable securities equal to $r - z$ are sold, returning the cash balance to z.

69

CHAPTER 14

ACCOUNTS RECEIVABLE AND INVENTORIES

14.1 SCOPE OF CREDIT MANAGEMENT

Credit management involves the development and implementation of policies on credit standards, credit terms and collections.

Credit policies involve evaluating the benefits of easing credit policies versus the costs of the low standards. Typically, easing standards will result in increased sales, increased investment in accounts receivable and increased bad debt losses.

Credit policy needs to reflect changing economic conditions as they affect both the firm and its customers.

14.2 CREDIT STANDARDS

A credit standard is the minimum criteria for the extension of credit to a customer.

One method of developing a credit standard is to establish credit risk classes based upon an estimate of probable loss ratio for each customer.

Credit scoring using discrimination analysis is used by large firms with a high volume of consumer accounts to establish credit standards.

14.3 CREDIT ANALYSIS

Credit managers frequently use the five "C's" of credit in evaluating the customer. These are:

1. Character — moral factor. Does the customer pay his bills?
2. Capacity — ability to pay, based upon management ability.

3. Capital — financial condition of the firm — ratio analysis.
4. Collateral — possible assets to be pledged.
5. Conditions — economic conditions and how they will affect the firm.

Credit information is gathered on the potential customer. Among the sources of such information are financial statements, Dun and Bradstreet, credit interchange bureaus, direct credit information exchanges and bank checking on customer balances.

Subjective judgment of the customer by an experienced analyst is a key input.

14.4 CREDIT TERMS

Credit terms include credit period, cash discounts and maximum credit line. These choices are important for monitoring the account and controlling the losses.

Cash discounts are designed to encourage early payment of the account. Terms 2/10 net 30 means the customer will receive a discount of 2% if the bill is paid within 10 days; if not, the entire bill is due in 30 days. This is an effective interest rate of 37%.

14.5 MONITORING ACCOUNTS RECEIVABLE

Three approaches used to monitor accounts receivable are listed below:

1. Average collection period or days sales outstanding.

Accounts receivable ÷ average daily sales

This measure is used by external analysts of a firm who do not have access to internal data. It can be estimated but is not as accurate as measures using internal data.

2. Aging schedule of accounts receivable. For each customer, outstanding receivables according to month purchased are posted.

This schedule is frequently required by banks from their loan customers and is superior to average collection period in evaluating accounts receivable. The accuracy of this measure can be affected by changing sales levels.

3. Payments Pattern Approach. Superior to average collection pe-

riod or aging schedule approach because it is unaffected by changes in level of sales. Accounts receivable are related to sales in the month of origin rather than to the average over a longer period.

Computers can be programmed to monitor the accounts and alert the credit manager to past due accounts and accounts where the credit limit is exceeded.

14.6 COLLECTION POLICIES

Policies must be established regarding when to use each collection technique. The basic techniques usually followed are: letters, telephone calls, personal visits, collection agencies and legal action.

While this is the basic order in which these techniques are used, many firms select only some of the techniques and may apply them differently with different customers. Size of customer, potential annual sales to the customer, size of outstanding receivable, and economic conditions are among the factors considered when deciding which techniques to use.

14.7 INVENTORY MANAGEMENT CONSIDERATIONS

There are three general types of inventory that need to be considered in developing an inventory control system: raw materials, work-in-process and finished goods. They are subject to differing constraints.

Raw-materials inventories are held to insure that production does not need to be interrupted due to lack of raw materials. Stability of supply, including transportation, is an important consideration.

Work-in-process inventory levels are primarily determined by the length of the production process. Sub-assemblies produced by other firms for inclusion in the finished product can be controlled by the same approach used for raw materials.

Finished-goods inventory control represents a trade-off with the marketing department who wish to be able to complete sales without delay.

14.8 ABC INVENTORY CONTROL SYSTEM

The ABC System is especially useful for control of finished goods inventory and for wholesaling and retailing firms.

"A" inventory items account for 70 percent of the inventory investment but only 20 percent of the items numerically. These items should be tightly controlled.

"B" inventory items account for 20 percent of the inventory investment but about 30 percent of the items. These warrant "average" control.

"C" inventory items account for only 10 percent of the inventory value but account for 50 percent of the items. Loose control of "C" inventory is appropriate. There may be "C" items, however, that are of a critical nature and these should be controlled closely to prevent stockout.

14.9 JUST-IN-TIME INVENTORY SYSTEM

Major manufacturing firms, such as autos and heavy equipment manufacturers, require their suppliers to carry the inventory and deliver it to the manufacturing plant on the day needed.

Suppliers usually locate in close proximity to the manufacturer to minimize transportation time. This strategy reduces the inventory investment for the manufacturer and shifts the cost to the supplier.

14.10 ECONOMIC ORDERING QUANTITY (EOQ) MODEL

The EOQ model seeks to minimize the total cost of inventory, which is defined as the sum of order costs and carrying costs.

Order costs include the clerical cost of placing and receiving an order. These costs are the cost of writing a purchase order, processing the paperwork, receiving the order and checking it against the invoice. These costs are essentially a fixed cost per order and do not vary by value of order and only to a limited extent by size of order. They are usually stated as dollars per order.

Carrying costs are the variable costs per unit of holding an item in inventory for a period of time. These costs include storage costs, insurance cost, deterioration and obsolescence and financing cost. Various studies have concluded that the cost of carrying inventory for one year is between 20% and 30% of the value of the inventory. These costs are usually stated as dollars per unit per period.

Graphic presentation of EOQ:

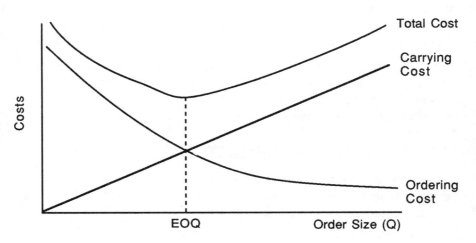

Optimal Order Quantity (Q)

$$Q^* = \sqrt{\frac{2SO}{C}}$$

where:
    S = usage in units per period
    O = order cost per order
    C = carrying cost per unit per period
    Q = order quantity in units

CHAPTER 15

SHORT-TERM FINANCING

15.1 SPONTANEOUS SOURCES OF CREDIT

One spontaneous source of credit is that of Trade Credit. The credit terms under which a firm purchases raw materials or finished goods inventory from its suppliers may be a significant source of credit. The following are some credit terms used:

Net period is the most frequently used type of credit term and is stated as "net 30 days," "net 45 days" or a similar period. The account is payable in full in the number of days from the invoice date.

A cash discount is given if the invoice is paid in full within the discount period. For example, 2/10, n/30 means that the face of the invoice can be discounted 2% if paid in full within 10 days of the invoice date; otherwise, the full amount of the invoice is due in 30 days of the invoice date.

Failure to take discounts is expensive. Under 2/10, n/30, failure to take the discount means you pay 2% interest for using the money 20 days or an annual interest rate of approximately 37%.

360 days ÷ 20 days = 18 × 2% = 37% with compounding.

Cash on Delivery (C.O.D.) — Sometimes new businesses or businesses with poor credit rating are not extended credit.

Cash Before Delivery (C.B.D.) — C.B.D. occurs in situations of poor credit rating where the customer may not have the cash and may refuse delivery. Seller then must pay round trip shipping and handling costs. Therefore, the customer is required to pay before shipping.

Seasonal Dating — This method is used by manufacturers, such as toy, which have a large seasonal demand. Goods are shipped early but payment terms are postponed until the selling season. By encouraging early purchase, production can be leveled and early shipment shifts inventory carrying costs to buyer.

Consignments — Goods are shipped but title remains with the shipper until goods are sold. The goods can be returned to shipper if unsold. This is used if seller wishes to get a new item on display or wishes to have a big sale on the item.

There are four main factors that influence the length of the credit period. They are:

1. **Economic nature of the product** — Products with high sales turnover usually have relatively short credit terms. Terms on fruits and vegetables may run 15 – 30 days. Credit on goods with slow turnover, such as jewelry, may run six months or longer.

2. **Seller Circumstances** — Financially weak suppliers may require cash or very short credit terms.

3. **Buyer circumstances** — Financially sound retailers who sell on credit receive relatively long terms from suppliers. Retailers selling in particularly risky industries, such as clothing, receive extended terms but are offered large discounts to encourage early payments.

4. **Cash Discounts** — See p. 75.

Net Credit is the difference between total accounts receivable and total accounts payable. Large, well-financed firms tend to be net suppliers of trade credit and underfinanced firms of all sizes tend to be net users of trade credit.

Accruals — Accrued expenses, such as accrued wages and accrued taxes, are sources of short-term, interest-free credit.

Customers sometimes partially prepay the cost of a major purchase. This is more common where the item is of large value, custom-built to specifications and requires a longer production time.

15.2 NEGOTIATED CREDIT – SOURCES

The main sources of short-term negotiated credit are commercial banks, commercial finance companies and factors. (Factors are firms who specialize in purchasing commercial accounts receivable. Factoring started in the textile industry but has become more widely accepted in recent years.) This chapter will concentrate on banks; however, many commercial finance companies have purchased factors and many factors have purchased finance companies, thus, either one can provide the full range of secured financing.

15.3 CHOOSING A BANK

A potential borrower should recognize that banks differ in several respects. Some investigation prior to requesting a loan may result in a more satisfactory long-term relationship.

One such difference is that banks have different policies toward risk. Banks also differ in their ability or willingness to work with new firms. Some banks develop expertise in certain industries, such as fish processing, and some may be more creative in developing financing. Some banks may have a venture financing subsidiary or may assist in locating equity financing.

Banks may also differ in their degree of loyalty to a customer in different times, in their degree of deposit stability, and in their degree of loan specialization.

The size of the bank can be important. Their lending limits are determined by their capital.

Banks differ in the variety of services that they can provide their business customers.

15.4 BANK LOANS — GENERAL

Self-Liquidating Loans – Banks are a major source of seasonal loans where the sale of the inventory and collection of the receivables provide the means of repaying the loan.

Single Payment Note — A single payment note is a loan for a specific purpose, not a recurring need. Maturity is usually 30 days up to 9 months or more.

Prime Rate is the lowest rate charged by leading national banks to their largest and most credit worthy customers. Banks use the prime as a base and adjust upward for risk. A specific customer, for example, might borrow at prime +2, meaning 2% over prime.

Fixed or Floating Rates — Loans may be set a specified (fixed) rate for the life of the loan or may change (float) as the prime rate changes.

Lines of Credit — A bank agrees for a specific time period, usually one year, to loan up to the amount agreed upon. This is **not a guaranteed loan** but instead, if the bank has sufficient funds available, it will allow the firm to borrow up to that amount. The line of credit agreement usually contains some restrictions on the customer. This loan is used for seasonal needs.

Annual Cleanup — To insure that the loan is for seasonal needs and not permanent working capital, the agreement may require that the firm completely repay the line of credit loan for one to two months each year.

Compensating Balances — As a provision of a line of credit or other business borrowing, the bank may require the customer to maintain bank balances equal to a specified percent, usually 10% – 20%, of the loan on deposit. If this deposit is larger than the customer would normally maintain, the effective cost of the loan is increased. Banks normally do not require compensating balances for small, underfunded businesses.

Revolving Credit Agreement — This is similar to a line of credit except that it is a guaranteed loan. Since the bank guarantees the availability of the loan, a commitment fee is normally charged. This fee is usually about .5 percent of the average unused balance of the loan.

Cost of Loans — Interest on loans is calculated in one of three ways, as shown below. The method used in calculating the interest may cause the **effective or true interest rate** to vary considerably from the **stated rate.**

1. **Regular, or Simple, Interest** — If interest is paid at maturity, the stated rate and effective interest rate are identical.

$$\text{Effective Rate} = \frac{\text{Interest}}{\text{Borrowed Amount}} = \frac{\$10,000}{\$100,000} = 10\%$$

2. **Discounted Interest** — Sometimes the interest is deducted at the beginning, reducing the amount received.

$$\text{Effective Rate} = \frac{\text{Interest}}{\text{Borrowed Amount} - \text{Interest}} = \frac{\$10,000}{\$90,000} = 11.1\%$$

3. **Installment Loan** — If the loan is repaid in 12 monthly payments, the principal is reduced by each monthly payment and thus the borrower has full use of the original principal for only one month.

Toward the end of the year, very little principal remains for use, thus, as an estimate, on an amortized loan, the borrower has an average of one-half the principal for use over the full year. Assuming interest is calculated on the original balance, the effective rate on average amount is thus:

$$\frac{10,000}{(100,000 \div 2)} = \frac{10,000}{50,000} = 20\%$$

Under the discounting method, the rate is even higher.

Effective rate on discount installment loan =

$$\frac{10,000}{[(100,000 - 10,000) \div 2]} = \frac{10,000}{45,000} = 22.7\%$$

15.5 COMMERCIAL PAPER

Commercial paper consists of promissory notes of large firms. It is sold primarily to other business firms, banks, insurance companies and pension funds. It is limited to firms with good credit risk. Dealers prefer to handle the paper of firms with at least $100 million of net worth and annual borrowing of at least $20 million.

Paper of business firms is sold through commercial paper dealers with maturities of 30 days to 270 days. Over 270 days would require registration with the SEC.

Finance companies sell their paper direct and will tailor the maturity to fit the investment needs of the buyer, up to 270 days. Finance company paper may be issued with only a few days to maturity.

Commercial paper will carry an interest rate higher than the CD rate but typically below the prime rate.

15.6 USE OF COLLATERAL IN SHORT-TERM FINANCING

Many businesses borrow on an unsecured basis. This is preferable because of reduced paperwork and increased flexibility. Many firms, however, do not have the option of borrowing without collateral.

Many assets may be used for collateral. Marketable securities, land, buildings, inventory and accounts receivable are all used. Few firms hold a marketable securities portfolio of sufficient size to use as collateral and real estate is normally used for long-term financing. Accounts receivable and inventory are the common forms of collateral for short-term borrowing.

15.7 ACCOUNTS RECEIVABLE AS COLLATERAL

There are three methods for using accounts receivable as collateral — general lien, pledging and factoring.

A **general lien** may be taken against all receivables without attempting to determine their quality. This may be coupled with a lien against inventory. This is the simplest form but provides the least security.

Pledging of accounts receivable requires a specialized bank department or the use of a collateral control company. Commercial finance companies pioneered this form. Pledging involves acceptance of individual customer accounts and control of balances by the bank. Title does not pass, it is usually on a non-notification basis and is with recourse.

Factoring is the sale of accounts receivable to the factoring subsidiary of a bank or to a factor. The factor evaluates each account prior to accepting them. Sale is usually on a notification basis and is without recourse.

15.8 INVENTORY AS COLLATERAL

Floating or Blanket Inventory Lien — This is a general lien against all inventory, with no attempt to value or identify it. Usually the loan will be low in relation to the book value of the inventory.

Chattel Mortgage — Inventory items must be specifically identified by serial number or other means and cannot be sold without the consent of the lender.

Trust Receipt Loans — This arrangement, also called floor planning, is used for inventories that can be individually identified by serial number or other means. It is extensively used to finance inventories by automobile dealers and appliance dealers. The borrower holds in trust for the lender the inventory and proceeds from the sale of the inventory.

Warehouse Receipt Loans — Warehouse receipt loans may use terminal or public warehouses or a field warehouse may be used. A field warehouse belongs to the borrower but is under the control of the lender. Inventory placed in the warehouse is given a warehouse receipt which is held by the lender as collateral against the loan.

Bankers Acceptances — A form of inventory financing based upon a bank letter of credit and used for international trade or domestic goods in transit or storage. The bank draft for the purchase price of the inventory is "accepted" by the buyer's bank. This bankers acceptance becomes a marketable security.

Bill of Lading — When goods are shipped, a bill of lading is generated which must be presented to claim the goods from the carrier. The bill of lading is sometimes used as collateral for a loan when goods are in transit.

Collateral Certificates — Certificates issued by a collateral control firm to verify the existence and value of the inventory may be used as security for a bank loan. The inventory is on the premises of the borrower but is not physically segregated. It is controlled by bonded employees of the collateral control firm and the value of the inventory is established by an agreed formula.

CHAPTER 16

CAPITAL MARKETS AND COMMON STOCK FINANCING

16.1 SOURCES OF BUSINESS FINANCING

In making decisions regarding sources of financing, firms would consider the following three major sources:

1. Long-term internal source based on retained earnings and depreciation.

2. Long-term external source.

3. Short-term external source.

Another important consideration in a financing decision is whether to raise funds privately or publicly.

Private financing is obtained directly from individuals, financial institutions, or non-financial corporations. It is also called direct financing or private placement. The advantages of this type of financing are: speed, flexibility and low issuance costs.

Public financing is obtained indirectly from individuals, financial institutions, or non-financial corporations through the utilization of the expertise of investment bankers.

16.2 INVESTMENT BANKING

In addition to rendering brokerage services, investment bankers or underwriters buy new issues from corporations and governments and then they sell them to the public.

16.2.1 FUNCTIONS OF THE INVESTMENT BANKER:

1. Advisory — The underwriter will advise corporations whether or not to issue new securities, what type of securities should be issued, whether or not to merge, etc.

2. Administrative — The investment banker will investigate and prepare the issue documents according to the security laws and SEC regulations.

3. Underwriting — The investment banker guarantees that the issuer of the new securities will receive a certain minimum amount of cash for its new securities should the market conditions change. Not all new security issues are underwritten. In this case, the investment banker may arrange for direct **private placement** or agree to sell the shares in a **public offering** on a **best effort basis** while assuming no responsibility if all the securities cannot be sold.

4. Distribution — Capitalizing on their reputation, connections, and distribution networks, investment bankers will sell the issue directly or indirectly to the public.

16.2.2 THE INVESTMENT BANKING PROCESS:

Stage I — The firm decides preliminarily on: how much external funds are needed; what type and classes of securities to use; whether to use competitive bids or negotiated deals; and if negotiated, which one of the investment bankers to select.

Stage II — A pre-underwriting conference is arranged between the issuing firm and the investment banker to re-evaluate the initial decisions made by the firm in Stage I. They also negotiate the terms of the underwriting agreement.

Stage III — A registration statement and prospectus containing financial and business information of the firm is filed with the SEC. During this period the investment bankers are not allowed to offer the securities for sale.

Stage IV — The investment banker sets the offering price taking into account the current market price of the stock (or the yield on the bonds), demand and supply, and the life cycle of the firm. The right price is one that is not too low; this would be costly to the firm. It also cannot be too high; this might cause losses for the underwriters.

Stage V — If the issue is sizeable, the investment banker (the originator, lead, or managing underwriter) forms an underwriting syndicate made up of other investment bankers, dealers and brokers to spread the risk with the purchase and distribution of the issue.

Stage VI — During the period of public offering, the investment banker must stabilize the price of the issue to prevent its drifting downward.

16.3 COMMON STOCK FINANCING

Advantages of common stock financing:

— It generally does not entail required fixed charges.

— There is no fixed maturity.

— It increases the creditworthiness and the borrowing power of the firm.

— It appeals to investors because it is a good inflation hedge.

— It appeals to investing corporations because 70 percent of the dividends received by one corporation from another is excluded from taxable income.

Disadvantages of common stock financing:

— It can dilute the existing ownership positions of current stockholders.

— The cost of underwriting and distribution are usually higher than those for preferred stocks or bonds.

— Dividends are not tax deductible.

— If more equity is infused beyond the optimal capital structure, the average cost of capital will be higher.

The Market for Common Stock — Some companies are privately owned (closely held), and some are publicly owned. Stocks of closely held companies are listed on the over-the-market (OTC) while publicly owned companies are either listed on an organized exchange(s) or the OTC. Stocks can be sold in the primary or secondary markets.

Advantages of going public:

— The founders can diversify their holdings.

— It will increase liquidity.

— It is easier to raise cash.

— It is easier to establish a firm's value in the market.

Disadvantages of going public:

— It is more costly to file reports with the SEC.

— The company must disclose more information, thus weakening competition.

— Self-dealings are harder to get.

— If the company is very small, its stock might be illiquid.

— Due to takeover activities, it is difficult to maintain ownership control.

16.4   REGULATION OF SECURITY MARKETS

SEC is the federal agency which regulates the stock and bond markets by overseeing all interstate offerings of new issues in amounts of $1.5 million or more and approves the registration statement and prospectus. The SEC regulates all organized exchanges and security fraudulent activities including insider trading.

The Board of Governors of the Federal Reserve system controls the **margin requirements** which indicate the maximum percentage of borrowing that investors can use to buy a stock.

Under the **blue sky laws**, states control the issuance of new securities within their boundaries. These laws were enacted to keep deceitful individuals or institutions from selling securities that offered the "blue sky" but which actually had little or no security backing.

The National Association of Securities Dealers (NASD) works with the SEC to regulate the over-the-counter (OTC).

CHAPTER 17

DEBT AND PREFERRED STOCK FINANCING

17.1 CHARACTERISTICS OF LONG-TERM DEBT

Advantages to debtholders:

— It is less risky than stocks because debtholders have prior claim on assets and earnings in case of the firm's liquidation.

— Except in the case of income bonds, debtholders have assurance of fixed income.

— The borrower is required to provide financial statements, pay taxes and other liabilities, and meet the restrictive covenants.

Disadvantages to debtholders:

— It is not a good inflation hedge.

— Debtholders do not participate in superior earnings.

— Debtholders do not have voting power.

Advantages to the corporation:

— Debtholders do not participate in superior earnings.

— Debtholders do not have voting power.

— The interest on debt is tax deductible.

— In case of callable bond, the coupon rate is lower than in the case of a straight bond.

— The cost of debt is generally lower than the cost of preferred stock and almost always lower than the cost of common stock.

— Ownership positions of existing stockholders are not diluted.

Disadvantages to the corporation:

— Interest must be paid regardless of the level of income.

— It has to meet the restrictive contractual covenants at all times.

— The cost of long-term financing is generally higher than that of short-term financing.

— The higher the debt ratio the greater the financial risk and the lower the borrowing capacity of the firm.

— Unlike equity, debt capital is not permanent capital. If the business has a continuing need for capital, the debt must be refinanced.

17.2 DEBT INSTRUMENTS

A **Bond** is a long-term promissory notes.

A **Loan Note** is a signed document representing evidence of debt.

A **Note** is an intermediate-term bond.

A **Funded Debt** is a long-term debt.

An **Indenture** is a deed of trust containing the rights and obligations of the issuing firm and bondholders.

A **Trustee** is an agent who ensures that the provisions of the indenture are adhered to.

A **Sinking Fund Bond** is a bond requiring the issuing firm to retire a certain amount of the bond each year.

A **Callable Bond** is a bond allowing the issuing firm to call back the bond at price above par value. The difference is called call premium. The process is called bond refunding and its purpose is to save on interest cost by calling the old bond paying a high interest rate and issuing a new bond paying a lower interest rate.

Secured Bonds are bonds backed by a mortgage (mortgage bond), securities (collateral trust bond), personal property (equipment trust certificates), or any asset of the firm.

An **Unsecured Bond** is a bond that is not backed by a security (debenture). They are issued by large creditworthy firms.

Unlike a straight bond, an **income bond** does not pay interest to bondholders unless the firm generates sufficient income. Unpaid past interest is generally cumulative.

A **Zero Coupon Bond** is a bond that makes no periodic interest payment but instead is sold at a deep discount from its face value. The buyer of such a bond receives the rate of return by the gradual appreciation of the security, which is redeemed at face value on a specified maturity date.

A **Eurobond** is a bond issued in U.S. dollar but sold in foreign countries, or issued in Japanese yen but sold in foreign countries other than Japan, etc.

Foreign Bond are bonds denominated in U.S. dollars, issued by a foreign firm, and sold in the U.S. (Yankee Bond), or denominated in British pounds, issued by a non-British firm and sold in Britain (Bulldog Bond), etc.

Industrial Development Bonds are bonds issued by local governments to attract new industry. Unlike capital gains, interest is exempt from federal income tax.

A **Pollution Control Bond** is a bond issued by local governments. The proceeds from its sale are made available to industrial firms to help them finance the acquisition of equipment designed to protect the environment from pollution.

A **Variable-Rate Bond** is a bond whose coupon rate is not fixed. These bonds reduce the risk to the borrowing firm when the interest rate declines while it increases the risk for the lending institutions. The risk will shift when the interest rate increases.

Convertible Bonds are bonds that allow the investor to convert the bond into a stated number of shares of the firm's common stock. A Convertible bond is a callable bond. From the viewpoint of the firm, the financing cost of a convertible bond is lower than that of a straight bond. From the investor's viewpoint, convertible bonds provide fixed interest payments and ownership when converted to common stock.

A **Putable Bond** is a bond that can be redeemed at the bondholder's option. It can be exercised only if the issuing company takes some specified action, such as being acquired by a weaker company, etc.

An **Indexed Bond** is also known as a purchasing power bond. It is popular in countries with very high inflation rates such as Brazil and Israel. The interest rate on these bonds is based on an inflation index such as the consumer price index, so the interest paid rises when the inflation rate rises, thus protecting the bondholders against inflation.

Junk Bonds are bonds with a credit rating of BB or lower by rating agencies. Junk bonds are issued by companies without long track records of sales and earnings, or those with questionable credit strength. It is a high-risk, high-yield bond issued to finance mergers, leveraged buyouts, and troubled companies.

17.3 PREFERRED STOCK

Preferred Stock — Preferred stock is a security which pays fixed dividends. Preferred stock has claims and rights ahead of common stock but behind all bonds. Most preferred stock issues provide for cumulative dividends. Recently, most of the newly issued preferred stocks are convertible to common stock. Some types participate with the firm's stock in sharing the firm's earnings. Like bonds, some preferred stocks have a sinking fund requirement. Some are callable.

Investment Value of a Preferred Stock — The value of straight preferred stock is obtained by dividing the stated fixed dividends by the required rate of return. For a convertible preferred stock, the value is derived from two sources: the value of straight preferred stock and the value of conversion of the convertible preferred stock to common stock. The conversion value is equal to the market price of the straight preferred stock times the conversion ratio. The ratio is the term of exchange between preferred and common stocks.

Advantages to the corporation:

— The corporation is not obligated to pay dividends unless there are enough realized profits.

— Funds raised through preferred stock increase the equity capital and therefore increase the firm's borrowing capacity.

— By issuing preferred stock, the firm can avoid fixed debt repayment and interest payments, and therefore future cash flow would be greater than financing via debt.

— Ownership positions of existing shareholders are not diluted when preferred stock is issued.

— If the value of the firm increases, the benefits go to the common stockholders, not to the preferred stockholders, except with convertible and participating preferred stock.

— If the preferred stock does not have a mandatory redemption requirement, the preferred is permanent capital.

— Preferred allows the firm to avoid giving voting power to preferred stockholders.

— Unlike bonds, preferred stocks empower the firm to preserve mortgageable assets for use in an emergency.

— Compared to bonds, preferred with no maturity or sinking fund causes less cash flow problems.

Disadvantages to the corporation:

— Dividends paid are not tax deductible.

— Smaller firms cannot use preferred stock for financing unless there is an equity kicker, such as warrant or conversion to common stock.

— The required rate of return on a preferred stock is generally higher than the interest rate on debt.

Advantages to the investors:

— Preferred stockholders receive fixed assured income.

— In case of liquidation, preferred stockholders have senior position over common stockholders.

— Most of the dividends received by investing institutions are not taxable.

— In the case of convertible preferred, the investor can reap the benefits of common ownership and control when the preferred is converted into common stock.

Disadvantages to the investors:

— The return does not compensate for the ownership risk.

— Prices of preferreds fluctuate more than those of bonds.

— The issuing corporation is not obligated to pay dividends unless there is a realized profit.

— In case of cumulative preferreds, accrued dividends are seldom paid off in full after a firm has recovered from trouble.

CHAPTER 18

WARRANTS, CONVERTIBLES AND OPTIONS

18.1 WARRANTS

A **Warrant** is a security issued together with a bond or a preferred stock that entitles the holder to buy a proportionate amount of common stock at a specified price, within a specified period of time. Warrants are usually detachable, but not always.

In corporate financing, a warrant is usually issued as a sweetener, to enhance the marketability of the accompanying low-interest fixed income securities.

Warrants Versus Convertible Securities Financing:

— The company receives additional funds when warrants are exercised, whereas it does not when convertibles convert.

— The combination of warrant and bond is more flexible from the holder's standpoint than a convertible bond because there are two separate securities. From the firm's standpoint, warrants may provide less control than convertible securities because the firm cannot force holders of warrants to exercise them.

Value of Warrant:

$$W = N(P - E) \text{ if } P \text{ is greater than } E$$

$$\text{or } W = 0 \quad \text{if } P \text{ is equal or less than } E$$

where: N = the number of shares of common stock that can be purchased with one warrant,

P = the market price of the common stock,

E = the exercise price of the common stock.

Initial Value of a Bond With Warrants:

$$IV_B = V_B + V_W$$

where IV_B = initial value of the bond,
V_B = straight-debt value of bond
V_w = value of warrant

18.2 CONVERTIBLES

Convertibles are hybrid securities offering to investors some of the advantages of fixed-income securities, while at the same time providing an opportunity to participate in rising stock prices.

The **conversion ratio** is the ratio in which the convertible security can be exchanged for common stock.

The **conversion price** is calculated by dividing the par value of the convertible security by the conversion ratio.

Valuation of Convertible Securities — The value of a convertible bond is based on two things: the value of the straight bond, and the conversion value of the bond. The first is calculated as follows:

$$V_B = \sum_{t=1}^{N} \frac{I_t}{(1+K_d)^t} + \frac{P_n}{(1+K_d)^n}$$

where I_t = interest payment at the end of period t
P = principal payment
n = number of periods to maturity
K_d = yield to maturity

The **conversion value** of a convertible bond is equal to the market price of the common stock times the conversion ratio.

The **conversion premium** depends on the difference between the value of the straight bond and the conversion value of the bond.

Accounting Treatment – Converting a convertible security into common stock dilutes primary EPS, and reduces the debt/equity ratio. The current accounting procedures require reporting of two EPS figures: primary EPS and fully diluted EPS. The primary EPS is determined by dividing the net earnings by the average number of shares of common stock that would have been outstanding during the year if certain convertible securities had been converted. The fully-diluted EPS is determined by dividing net earnings by the average number of shares of common stock that would have been outstanding if all convertible securities had been converted.

Advantages of convertible financing:

— It provides for future common stock financing.

— It provides for a change in the capital structure of the company and would increase its future borrowing capacity.

— It provides for lower cost of financing.

— It provides a sweetener for financing.

18.3 OPTIONS

Call Option — A call option gives the right to buy an asset at a specified price within a specified period of a time. A put option is the right to sell an asset at a specified price within a specified period of time. The buyer of a call or a put has the right to exercise his/her option whereas the seller (writer) is obligated to deliver.

Option and Financing — Despite the fact that options are actively traded on options exchanges and they are well-known as investment securities, they play an insignificant role as a financing vehicle. However, the financial manager uses option or future contracts to hedge against possible future increases in the interest rate. If the company decided that they would need to issue a bond in six months and they are concerned about a possible increase in the interest rate, they would be either selling a call option or future contract on Treasury bonds. By doing so, the financial manager would lock-in the interest rate, avoiding borrowing at a higher cost.

CHAPTER 19

LEASING

19.1 TYPES OF LEASES

Operating Lease — An operating lease is also called a maintenance or service lease. This is a lease contract covering short or intermediate terms. Here the lessor, rather than the lessee, is responsible for maintenance, insurance, and taxes related to the leased asset. It is a cancellable contract with proper notice. Usually, operating leases are not fully amortized. Assets leased include computers, automobiles, and trucks.

Financial Lease — This is a lease contract covering intermediate or long terms. Here the lessee, rather than the lessor, is responsible for maintenance, insurance, and taxes related to the leased asset. It is a noncancellable contract. Usually, financial leases are fully amortized. Assets leased include land, buildings, and aircrafts.

Sale and Leaseback — In this type of lease company A sells an asset to company B, and company B (lessor) leases it back to Company A (lessee). Company A receives the sales price in cash and the economic use of the asset during the lease period. In turn, company A will make periodic lease payment to company B. In this case, company B realizes any salvage value.

Direct Leasing — In direct leasing a company acquires the economic use of the leased asset it did not own previously. For example, a company may lease a computer from a computer manufacturer such as International Business Machines.

Leveraged Leasing — There are three parties involved in leasing: the lessee, the lessor, and the lender. The lessee uses the asset and makes the periodic lease payments. The lessor owns the asset which is financed in part by a long-term lender. The lessor is both an equity participant and a borrower.

19.2 FINANCIAL STATEMENT EFFECTS

Financial Accounting Standards Board's rule (FASB) No. 13 distinguishes between **capital lease** and **operating lease**. If the lessee acquires all of the economic benefits and risks of the leased asset (capital lease), then the lessee must report the present value of the asset on the asset side of the balance sheet, and the lease obligations must be shown on the liability side of the balance sheet. If the lessee does not acquire all the economic benefits and risks of the leased asset (operating lease), then it can be shown in footnotes to the balance sheet. The latter case is called off-balance sheet lease financing.

According to FASB No. 13, the amortization of the leased asset and the annual interest which is part of the annual lease payment should be deductible as an expense. In an operating lease, only the lease payment is deductible as an expense.

19.3 LEASING VS. BORROWING

Sometimes firms face the problem of deciding whether they should lease the asset or purchase it and finance the purchase by borrowing. In general, whether lease financing or borrowing is favored will depend on the patterns of cash outflows for each financing method, and the opportunity cost of the funds.

Steps that should be taken to decide whether to lease or to borrow:

1. Evaluate the project using one of the discounted cash flow methods: NPV or IRR.

2. Decide whether the project should be financed by debt or lease. This is done by comparing the cost of debt to the cost of lease financing.

3. If a firm is in a field where the products change rapidly, such as telecommunications or computer industries, it may not have the option of a long-term lease, but would have to compare a short-term lease against purchasing the equipment outright.

EXAMPLE:

Consider that ABC Company has decided to purchase equipment

costing $200,000. If it were to lease finance the equipment, the lessor will provide such financing over 10 years. The lease payments are made in advance, i.e, at the end of the year prior to each of the 10 years. The depreciable life of the equipment is 10 years, and the company uses the straight line method of depreciation. The salvage value is zero and the amortization of the lease is 10 years, the lessor requires 8 percent return, the borrowing interest rate is 10 percent, and the tax rate is 50 percent. If the company buys the equipment, it will get a trade a discount of 10 percent. Use the NPV to determine whether the company should borrow or purchase the equipment.

SOLUTION:

Step 1: Calculate the annual lease payments X:
This is an annuity-due case
$$\$200,000 = X \, (PVIFA_{.08,10}) \, (1 + .08)$$
$$X = \$27,598.$$

Step 2: Calculate the present value (PV) of the cash outflows associated with the lease alternative:

End of Year	(1) Lease Payments	(2) Tax Shield (1)(.5)	(3) Cash Outflows After Taxes (1) – (2)	(4) PV of Cash Outflows .10(1–.5)=.05
0	$27,598	—	$27,598	$ 27,598
1–9	27,598	$13,799	13,799	98,081
10	—	13,799	(13,799)	(8,471)
				$117,208

Step 3: Calculate the annual loan payments, LP, (interest and principal). Assume that loan payments are made at the beginning of the year.
$$\$200,000 \, (1-.10) = \$180,000$$
$$\$180,000 = LP \, (PVIFA_{.10, 10})(1 + .10)$$
$$LP = \$26,631$$

Step 4: Calculate the annual interests on the loan:

End of Year	Annual Payments (inter. + prin.)	Principal Amount Owing at End of Year	Annual Interest
0	$26,631	$153,369*	0
1	26,631	142,075**	$15,337
2	26,631	129,652	14,208**
3	26,631	115,986	12,965
4	26,631	100,954	11,599
5	26,631	84,418	10,095
6	26,631	66,229	8,442
7	26,631	46,221	6,623
8	26,631	24,212	4,622
9	26,631	0	2,421

* $180,000 – $26,631 = $153,369
$153,369 (.10) = $15,337
** $26,631 – $15,337 = $11,294
$153,369 – $11,294 = $142,075
$142,075 (.10) = $14,208

Step 5:   Calculate the present value (PV) of the cash outflows associated with the borrowing alternative:

End of Year	(1) Loan Payment	(2) Interest	(3) Deprec.	(4) Tax Shield	(5) Cash Outflow After Tax	(6) PV@.05
0	$26,631	0	0	0	$26,631	$26,631
1	26,631	$15,337	20,000	$17,669	8,962	8,535*
2	26,631	14,208	20,000	17,104	9,527	8,641**
3	26,631	12,965	20,000	16,483	10,148	8,766
4	26,631	11,599	20,000	15,800	10,831	8,911
5	26,631	10,095	20,000	15,048	11,583	9,076
6	26,631	8,422	20,000	14,221	12,410	9,261
7	26,631	6,623	20,000	13,312	13,319	9,466
8	26,631	4,622	20,000	12,311	14,320	9,692
9	26,631	2,421	20,000	11,211	15,422	9,941
10	0	0	20,000	10,000	(10,000)	(6,139)
						$102,781

*   loan payment - tax shield

$8,962 (PVIF$_{.05,1}$) = $8,535

** $9,527 (PVIF$_{.05,2}$) = $8,641

Columns (1) and (2) are carried forward from step 4. Column (3) is the straight-line depreciation. Column (4) equals the sum of columns (2) and (3), times the tax rate. Column (5) equals column (1) minus column (4). Column (6) equals column (5) times the present value interest factor.

Step 6: Compare the present value (PV) of cash outflows in step 2 with the PV of cash outflows in step 5. Since the latter is less than the former, the company should purchase the equipment through debt financing.

CHAPTER 20

DIVIDEND POLICY

20.1 CONSIDERATIONS IN DIVIDEND POLICY

Dividend Policy – The dividend policy determines whether to pay out or not to pay out cash dividends to stockholders. If it is decided to pay out, dividend policy involves the determination of the payout and retention ratios.

Record Date — This is the date on which a stockholder must own shares in order to receive dividends.

Ex-Dividend — When a stock sells ex-dividend, i.e., prior to the record date, buyers do not receive dividends.

Payment Date — The payment date is the actual date on which the firm will pay dividends to the holders of record.

Implications — We are interested in dividend policy because it affects the firm's stock price. In the short run, increasing the dividend payout would increase the price. In the long run, however, increasing the payout would deprive the company of sources of funds for reinvestment, hamper the growth of the firm, and depress the stock price. One of the functions of the financial manager is to tailor an optimal dividend policy to maximize the value (stock price) of the firm by striking a balance between the short and long run considerations.

20.2 DIVIDEND POLICY THEORIES

Dividend Irrelevance Theory — Miller and Modigliani's 1961 article shows mathematically that the stock price of the firm is determined mainly by the earning power of the firm's assets or its investment policy, and that whether to pay out or to retain earnings is irrelevant to stock valuation. The theory is based on the following assumptions: perfect capital markets; no flotation costs; no taxes; a constant investment policy; financial leverage does not affect the cost of capital; and earning payout or retention has no effect on the cost (required rate of return) of equity capital.

The Residual Theory of Dividends — The dividend payout will depend on the availability of profitable investment projects whose internal rate of return exceeds the required rate of return. If there were profitable investment projects, they should be financed from the earnings, and the dividend payout ratio should be small or zero. If there were no profitable investment projects, the dividend payout ratio should be 100 percent. This theory supports the irrelevance of dividend policy in the valuation of stock.

EXAMPLE:

ABC Company treats dividends as a residual decision. The expected net earnings are $2,000,000. The company has an all-equity capital structure. The cost of equity capital is 10 percent.

1. If the company has $1,500,000 in profitable investment projects whose expected return exceeds 10 percent, how much should be paid out in dividends?

2. If the company has $2,000,000 in profitable investment projects whose expected return exceeds 10 percent, how much should be paid out in dividends?

3. If the company has $3,000,000 in projects whose expected return exceeds 11 percent, how much should be paid out in dividends? What else should be done?

SOLUTION:

1. Since the internal rate of return is greater than the required rate of return, and the net earnings are greater than the required financing needs, the firm should pay out $500,000 in dividends.

2. Since the internal rate of return is greater than the required rate of return, and the net earnings is equal to the required financing needs, the firm should not pay out any dividends.

3. Since the internal rate of return is greater than the required rate of return, and the net earnings are less than the required financing

needs, the firm should not pay out any dividends. The company should raise an additional $1,000,000 by issuing a common stock (the company assumes all-equity capital).

"Bird-in-the-Hand" Theory — Recall the Gordon Model which states mathematically that the cost of equity capital $K_s = (D_1/P_0) + g$. Gordon and Lintner (1962) argue that stockholders would prefer the expected dividends yield D_1/P_0 over the expected capital gains yield, g, because the former is more certain to realize and thus less risky. Therefore, the firm's value would be maximized by a high dividend payout ratio.

Miller and Modigliani, however, argue that the cost of equity capital, K_s, is independent of dividend policy because investors do not differentiate between dividend yield and capital gains yield. They called the Gordon-Lintner argument the "bird-in-the-hand" theory.

20.3 FACTORS AFFECTING DIVIDEND POLICY

Legal Factors — Legally, cash dividends may not be paid out of the firm's capital stock. Further, dividends may not be paid out if the firm has overdue liabilities, or is legally insolvent or bankrupt.

Contractual Factors — Cash dividends may not be paid out if it violates the restrictive provisions as spelled out in the loan agreement, bond indenture, preferred stock agreement, or lease contract.

Liquidity — A cash dividend may not be paid out if it affects the cash (liquidity) needs of the firm.

Financial Requirements — If the firm is a growing firm and needs funds to finance its expansion, cash dividends payout should be conservative. In this case, earnings should be used to meet the needed financing.

Availability of External Funds — Given the firm's risk-return characteristics, dividend policy should take into account the firm's ability to raise funds externally. Not all firms have easy access to external financing.

Owner Investment Opportunities — The dividend policy should take into account the market rates of return on alternative investment opportunities. If the rates of return on these alternatives were higher than the firm's internal rate of return, the firm should payout all earnings in cash dividends.

The Informational Content (Signaling) — A stable dividend payout indicates to the stockholders that the firm is successful and worthwhile to invest in. The stock market views the firm's dividends as a source of information about the future prospects of the firm. The announcement of dividends gives a "signal" to the investors about the profitability of the firm.

Control — If a firm pays out substantial dividends, it may need to raise external capital at a later stage through the sale of stock in order to finance their profitable investment projects. In this case, the controlling interest of the stockholders may be diluted.

Tax Status — The tax status of the firm's stockholders is important to consider when they have high marginal tax rates. In this case they prefer low dividend payout ratio.

20.4 TYPES OF DIVIDEND POLICIES

Stable Dividend Per Share — Dividend per share is increased when the firm is confident that a higher dividend can be maintained in the future. This is a popular policy.

Constant Dividend Payout Ratio — This is a less popular policy. Firms pay a fixed percentage of net earnings as cash dividends each period.

Small, Regular Dividend Plus Extras — This represents a compromise between paying a stable dividend per share and maintaining a constant dividend payout ratio. Based on the firm's performance, an extra dividend may be paid out at the end of the period.

20.5 STOCK DIVIDENDS AND SPLITS

Stock dividends and stock splits are essentially a recapitalization of the firm's capital accounts. They are not cash dividends, and the stockholder's proportional ownership remains unchanged.

Stock dividends are paid out in common stock. The firm pays out stock dividends either to conserve cash, retain a greater portion of its earnings to finance profitable investment projects, or replace cash dividends because of financial problems.

The motives for a stock split are to broaden the market for the stock or reduce the price to more favorable margin.

The effects of stock dividends:

— New shares are issued, and the number of shares outstanding is increased by the same percentage of stock dividends. Stock par value remains unchanged. The value of the new shares is paid out from the retained earnings account and transferred to both common stock and the additional paid-in capital accounts.

— The total net worth remains unchanged.

— The earnings per share will be reduced by the same percentage of stock dividends.

— The proportion of total earnings available to common stockholders remains unchanged.

The effects of stock split:

— New shares are issued and the par value of the stock is cut in half in the case of a 2-for-1 split, in third in the case of a 3-for-1 split, etc.

— No transfer is made from retained earnings account.

— Earnings per share are cut in half in the case of a 2-for-1 split, in third in the case of a 3-for-1 split, etc.

— The market price of the stock will be cut in half in the case of a 2-for-1 split, in third in the case of a 3-for-1, etc.

20.6 STOCK REPURCHASES

Companies repurchase shares of their own common stock for one of the following reasons:

1. To adjust their capital structure.

2. To forestall hostile takeovers.

3. As an alternative to paying cash dividends.

There are different methods for stock repurchases:

1. Purchasing shares in the open market.

2. The company may make a tender offer to buy shares at certain price within a specified period of time.

3. Purchasing a block of shares on a negotiated basis.

Advantages:

— A stock repurchase would reduce the number of shares outstanding and increase the earnings per share, thus increasing the value of the stock.

— The company can use the excess cash to buy shares to cover executive stock options and warrants that would be exercised in the future.

— The company can use the excess cash to buy shares to cover the conversion of convertible securities.

Disadvantages:

— The IRS may view stock repurchase as a way of helping shareholders to evade paying taxes on dividends, and thus may make them liable to the accumulated earnings tax.

— The SEC may view stock repurchase as a price manipulation: inflating the current stock price in anticipation of offering of new stock.

CHAPTER 21

BUSINESS EXPANSION AND BUSINESS FAILURE

21.1 MERGERS, COMBINATIONS, CONSOLIDATIONS, AND TAKEOVERS

Mergers are combinations of two or more companies, or consolidations.

A **Merger or Statutory Merger** is a combination of two or more companies in which one company survives as a legal entity while the others cease to exist.

A **Consolidation or a Statutory Consolidation** occurs when a new company is formed to acquire the net assets of the combining companies who cease to exist as legal entities. Technically speaking, consolidation is not a merger, because none of the combining companies exists legally.

A **Horizontal Merger** is a merger combining direct competitors in the same product line.

A **Vertical Merger** is a merger combining customer and company or supplier and company.

A **Market Extension Merger** is a merger combining companies selling the same product in different markets.

A **Product Extension Merger** is a merger combining companies selling different but related products in the same market.

A **Conglomerate Merger** is a merger combining companies with none of the above relationships or similarities.

A **Friendly Takeover** is a merger of two companies that takes place through direct negotiation between the two managements and their board of directors.

A **Hostile Takeover** is a merger which occurs when the target company's management opposes the deal, and the acquiring company goes over their heads by making a tender offer to the stockholders.

A **Tender Offer** is an offer to buy shares of the target company at a certain price directly from the stockholders. Tender offer can be cash or stock tender. Instead of one tender offer, some bidders make a two-tier offer, with two prices.

The **Crown Jewel** is the most valued asset held by a target company. The divestiture of this asset is frequently a sufficient defense to discourage takeover.

The **Raider** is the person or company attempting the takeover of another company.

Greenmail is the premium paid by a targeted company to a raider in exchange for the raider's shares of the targeted company.

A **Golden Parachute** is a large payment made to a top executive of a target firm, should the merger result in the loss of his/her job. A golden parachute might include generous severance pay, stock options, or a bonus.

The **Maiden** is the target company towards which a takeover attempt is directed.

A **Poison Pill** is a provision giving stockholders other than those involved in a hostile takeover the right to purchase securities at a very favorable price in the event of a takeover.

Shark Repellants are the antitakeover measures. They include: a plea to existing shareholders to keep holding their shares; repurchasing shares of the stock; private placement of stock; golden parachutes; search for a more friendly acquirer; and initiating frustrating legal action.

A **Stripper** is a successful raider who sells off some of the assets of the target company once the target is acquired.

A **White Knight** is a merger partner (solicited by management of a target) who offers an alternative merger plan to that offered by the raider and who protects the target company from attempted takeover by the raider.

21.2 REASONS FOR MERGERS

The ultimate reason for combinations is to increase the market value of the firm by either increasing the earnings per share (or equivalently increasing the dividends per share) or decreasing the required rate of return through lowering the firm's risk, or both.

Other reasons may be operating economies (synergy), economies of scale, improved management, future prospects of growth, diversification, undervalued companies, tax-loss carry-forward, and personal reasons.

21.3 FINANCIAL EVALUATION OF MERGERS

Mergers can be analyzed from the perspectives of the acquiring and acquired companies. Theoretically speaking, merger represents a capital budgeting from the perspective of the acquiring company, and therefore the net present value of cash flows should be calculated. If the NPV is positive, the acquiring company should buy the target company.

However, mergers involve quantitative and nonquantitative estimation. For instance, decisions should be made about the growth and profit potential of specific product markets, the quality and personal motives of a company's management, diversification, geographic proximity, and the compatibility of the two merged companies.

The following discounted cash flow model is utilized in the evaluation of the financial feasibility of the merger:

$$\text{NPV} = \sum_{t=1}^{n} \frac{CF_t}{(1+K)^t} - CF_0$$

where: CF_t = the after-tax operating cash flows that will be generated from the target company.

CF_0 = the market price of all the cash and securities that would be paid by the acquiring company to acquire the target company. CF_0 may also include the market price of the liabilities of the target company that the acquiring company agreed to assume as a result of the merger.

K = the risk-adjusted discount rate. It may be the weighted-average required return of the acquiring company, target company, or both, depending on the nature of risk of the merger.

The following steps should be taken to determine whether the merger should be consummated or not:

1. Estimate the cash inflows based on the pro forma income statements of the target company.

2. Estimate the discount rate.

3. Calculate the NPV of the cash flows.

EXAMPLE:

In December 19X9, ABC Company was considering the purchase of XYZ Company. ABC estimated that it would be able to purchase XYZ's common stock for $100 million cash plus 2 million shares of ABC's stock, which is presently selling for $60 a share. In addition, ABC will assume XYZ's debt, which has a book value of $20 million because market interest rates are above 14 percent. If the merger is consummated, ABC will need $16 million per year in capital expenditure for the next three years 19X0–19X2, and the assets can be sold at $120 million at the end of 19X2.

Should ABC Company purchase XYZ company?

SOLUTION:

Step 1: ABC has estimated the cash inflows based on the following pro forma statements for the next three years 199X – 19x2 (million of dollars):

	1998	1999	2000
Sales	200	260	340
Cost of goods sold	116	160	220
Depreciation	20	26	34
Earnings before interest and taxes	64	74	86
Interest	14	14	14
Earnings before taxes	50	60	72
Taxes at 40 percent	20	24	28.8
Earnings after taxes	30	36	43.2

Step 2:   ABC Company has decided to use its own weighted average required rate of return of 14 percent as the risk-adjusted discount rate. This decision was based on the similarity between the betas of ABC and XYZ stocks. It also is based on the target capital structure which they would like to maintain when the merger is completely consummated.

Step 3:   Calculate the NPV:

CF_t = EBIT(1–Tax) + Depreciation – Capital expenditure
Cash inflows in 1998 = 64 (1 – .40) + 20 –16 = $42.4
Cash inflows in 1999 = 74 (1 – .40) + 26 –16 = $48.4
Cash inflows in 2000 = 86 (1 – .40) + 34 –16 = $55.6

CF_0 = Price of XYZ's stock + Price of ABC's stock
+ Capital expenditures: 100 + 60 + 16 = $176 million

NPV =

$$-\$176 + \frac{\$42.4}{(1+.14)} + \frac{\$48.4}{(1+.14)^2} + \frac{\$55.6}{(1+.14)^3} + \frac{\$120}{(1+.14)^3} = \$16.96$$

Since the NPV is positive, ABC Company should purchase XYZ Company.

21.4   LEVERAGED BUYOUTS, SPINOFFS AND CARVE OUTS

Leveraged Buyout (LBO) represents a purchase of a company or a subsidiary that is financed with debt. Sometimes called asset-based lending, the debt is secured by the assets of the target company. With LBO, all public stockholders are bought out and the company or business unit becomes private.

Leveraged Cashout (LCO) — Unlike the case of LBO, in LCO a publicly-traded company raises cash through increased leverage and then distributes this cash to stockholders. The public shareholders keep their shares. Often management and other insiders do not receive cash but take stock instead, thereby increasing their proportional ownership of the company.

A **Sell-Off** is a decision to sell the entire firm or a part of the firm such as a division, subsidiary, or a product line.

A **Spin-Off** is a decision to divest a business unit such as a standalone subsidiary or division. In a spin-off, the business unit is not sold for cash or securities. Rather, common stock in the unit is distributed to the stockholders of the company on a pro rate basis, after which the operation becomes a completely separate company.

An **Equity Carve-Out** is similar to a spin-off, but the common stock in the business unit is sold to the public.

Partial sell-off, spin-off, and equity carve-out are forms of **divestiture**.

The following discounted cash flow model is used to determine the financial feasibility of divestiture:

$$NPV = SP - \sum_{t=1}^{n} \frac{CF_t}{(1+K)^t}$$

where: SP = estimated selling price of the assets.
          CF_t = estimated incremental after-tax cash flows foregone as a result of selling the assets.
          K = risk-adjusted discount rate.

For the company to divest, the NPV should be positive.

21.5 BUSINESS FAILURE

Business failure, or **technical insolvency,** is created when a business doesn't have money to pay its bills. They still may have sales, and report some profitability, but not enough cash to cover all facets of an operating business.

The basic causes of business failure are generally attributed to mismanagement, or the inability of management to correct significant problems in the operation of the business. The problems can be listed as follows:

1. Inability to control costs in overhead (burden) administrative or product costs so that an adequate profit can be earned.

2. Failure to collect accounts receivables, or to control the cash investment in inventory.

3. Failure in marketing to reach customers, or to design a product that fulfills a market need.

4. Inability to produce a safe and quality product, which results in costly product replacement and lawsuits.

5. Inability of management to adjust to economic downturns.

21.6 VOLUNTARY SETTLEMENT

A **Voluntary Settlement** is arranged with creditors rather than legal bankruptcy proceedings. This may be used with either technical insolvency or bankruptcy.

An **Extension** is an arrangement with creditors where debts will be paid in full over an extended period. Frequently creditors will require cash payment for current purchases.

Composition is a partial cash settlement of all claims.

Creditor Control is when creditors take control of the operations of the firm until the claims are settled.

An **Assignment** is an arrangement for liquidating a firm under voluntary liquidation. Creditors agree on a third party, such as an adjustment bureau, to liquidate the assets. Voluntary liquidation is less costly than a court procedure.

21.7 COURT SUPERVISED REORGANIZATION AND LIQUIDATION

Bankruptcy Reform Act of 1978 is the legislation which governs bankruptcy in the U.S. at present.

Chapter 11 is the portion of the Act which outlines the procedures for reorganizing a failed or failing firm. If a firm cannot be reorganized into a viable firm, it is liquidated.

Chapter 7 is the portion of the act which details the procedures to be followed in liquidating a firm.

There are two basic types of reorganization petitions. A petition for reorganization can be filed by the debtor, with some exceptions. An outside party, usually a creditor, can file for involuntary reorganization. Certain conditions must be met in order for a creditor to file an involuntary petition against a firm.

A reorganization plan is developed and submitted to the court. The plan is reviewed by all parties concerned and hearings are held. The plan must be accepted by at least two-thirds of the dollar amount of claims and by two-thirds of the shares of the owner groups. If approved by the groups and confirmed by the court, the plan is put into effect.

In liquidation, a trustee is appointed by the court to oversee the disposal of assets and payment of claims.

Secured creditors have first claim against receipts from sale of the pledged assets. If sale receipts are inadequate to satisfy secured claims, the secured creditors become general creditors for the remainder of their claims. If sale receipts are in excess of secured claims, the excess is used to satisfy general creditors.

The Act establishes detailed priority of claims for unsecured creditors. The Court supervises the payment of claims from the disposal of assets based upon these priorities.

21.8 BANKRUPTCY COSTS

The entry of new firms and exit of inefficient firms is important to the efficient operation of our economy. There are costs, however, to this process.

Direct Costs of bankruptcy consist of the out-of-pocket fees that arise from the bankruptcy process. These include filing fees, attorney fees, referee and trustee fees, accounting and appraiser fees and auctioneer fees. This is just a partial list of the fees involved in a bankruptcy case.

Indirect Costs are the lost efficiency and revenue of the firm as creditors, customers, and employees begin to foresee bankruptcy. Creditors are reluctant to extend additional credit and deliveries may be delayed, customers may shop elsewhere, employee morale deteriorates and turnover may increase. This process is detrimental to the owners and creditors as assets are liquidated below book value.

CHAPTER 22

INTERNATIONAL FINANCE

22.1 INTERNATIONAL VS. TRADITIONAL FINANCE

The following are the major factors that distinguish international financial management from the traditional financial management:

— Cash flows are denominated in different foreign currencies. Since the exchange rates of these currencies fluctuate over time, there is a foreign exchange risk.

— Different countries have different tax and legal systems which complicate their financial implications. This is a source of tax and legal risks.

— Different countries have different cultures that affect their financial systems. For instance, capital structure and the equity capital concepts, are perceived differently in Japan than in the U.S.

— Most financial models are based on free competitive markets. However, some countries have adopted different economic systems having different financial implications to financial modelling.

— Different countries have different political systems. The implications are that some countries might exercise their sovereign right to expropriate assets of the firm without compensation. Also, some countries have restrictions on currency remittances to the parent company. These examples represent sources of political, country, or sovereign risk.

— Different countries have different inflation rates. The excessive inflation rates in some countries represents a source of inflation risk.

22.2 EXCHANGE RATES AND MONETARY SYSTEMS

Foreign Exchange Rate is the price of one currency in terms of another. The rate may be quoted in terms of the number of dollars required to buy one unit of a foreign currency (direct quotation), or may be quoted in terms of the number of units of foreign currency to buy one U.S. $ (indirect quotation).

According to the Fixed Exchange System (Bretton Woods), the exchange rate of a currency was fixed in terms of the U.S. dollar which was tied to the value of gold. Member countries had to maintain the exchange rate of their currency within + 1% and − 1% of the specified fixed rate.

Implications of Bretton Woods:

— Under this system, exchange rates did not fluctuate frequently, and therefore, multinational corporations (MNCs) encountered lower exchange risk and were able to plan with more certainty.

— However, under this system, economic problems of different trading partners were more contagious, high inflation and unemployment rates in one country were known to lead to high inflation and unemployment rates in another.

Reasons for the Collapse of Bretton Woods:

— Many countries whose relative inflation rates were very high started to devalue their currencies relative to the U.S. dollar.

— Because of the role of the U.S. dollar, the $ was overvalued, and the U.S. balance of payment deficit worsened.

— There was a shortage of gold in the world, particularly in the U.S.

Important Events:

— August 1971 — Because of a high inflation rate, President Nixon decided that the dollar should be devalued against other currencies, and the U.S. stopped buying or selling gold for dollars.

— December 1971 — The Smithsonian Agreement was signed. It called for the devaluation of the dollar by 7.9% against other currencies. Also, member governments should intervene when exchange rate exceeds +2.25% or falls below −2.25% of the original par values of its currency.

114

- April 1972 — Led by Germany, the Snake Agreement was signed by a number of European countries to form a currency union with fixed rates between members but floating rates relative to all other countries.

- February 1973 — Devaluation of the dollar and the end of the Smithsonian Agreement led to the demise of the international fixed exchange system.

- October 1976 — The joint meetings of the International Monetary Fund (IMF) and the World Bank in Jamaica decided to abrogate the fixed exchange system, leading the way to the emergence of the floating exchange system. Here the gold was demonetized, and the special drawing rights (SDRs) were created to replace gold.

- March 1979 — The Snake collapsed and the European Monetary System (EMS) was created. Under the EMS, exchange rates of member countries are held together within specified limits, and are also tied to the European Currency Unit (ECU).

Under the Floating Exchange System, direct government intervention is minimal and foreign exchange rates are determined mainly by market forces, i.e., by the demand and supply which are functions of:

- Demand for and supply of tradeable goods
- Relative inflation rates in different countries
- Relative interest rates in different countries
- Relative income levels in different countries
- International investments
- Speculation

Implications of the Floating Exchange System:

- Exchange rates fluctuate more frequently which would create foreign exchange risk for MNCs and would make financial planning more cumbersome.

- However, economic problems of different trading partners may not be contagious.

Under the Dirty Float system, exchange rates are technically floating but not freely. Governments sometimes intervene directly or indirectly to affect rates.

22.3 THE FOREIGN EXCHANGE MARKETS

Spot (Cash) Market is a market which contains dealers and traders who trade in foreign currencies for immediate delivery. The relevant rates are the spot rates.

Forward Market is a market which contains dealers and traders who trade in foreign currencies for future delivery. Future and forward contracts are used for this purpose. Future contracts are more standardized in terms of the size and the duration of the contract.

Eurocurrency Market — Eurocurrency is a currency held in the form of time deposits in financial institutions outside the home country of the currency, e.g., Eurodollar is a U.S. dollar-denominated time deposit which is deposited outside the U.S.; Euroyen is a Japanese yen denominated time deposit which is deposited outside Japan, etc.

Cross Rate is the rate that is derived from the foreign exchange rates of two currencies. The cross rate of currency "A" relative to currency "B" is the dollar value of currency "A" divided by the dollar value of currency "B".

Discount Versus Premium — When the forward rate of a currency is higher than the spot rate, it is said that the currency is selling at premium. When forward rate is lower than the spot rate, it is said that the currency is selling at discount.

The annualized discount/premium (D/P) is calculated using the following formula:

$$\frac{D}{P} = \frac{\text{Forward rate} - \text{Spot rate}}{\text{Spot rate}} \times \frac{12}{n} \times 100$$

where: n = number of months forward i.e. duration of the forward contract.

22.4 THEORIES OF INTERNATIONAL FINANCE

Covered Interest Arbitrage involves investing in a time deposit at a foreign country whose currency interest rate is higher than the interest rate on local currency deposits, and concurrently covering the position by selling a future contract maturing at the same time of the time deposit. In this situation you arbitrage the interest rates and cover your position against possible devaluation or depreciation of the foreign currency.

Interest Rate Parity states that the currency premium or discount is determined by the differential in interest rates between the two countries. As a result, covered interest arbitrage will not be profitable. Mathematically, it is expressed as follows:

$$P = \frac{(1 + i_h)}{(1 + i_f)} - 1$$

where P = the premium/discount,

               i_h = the interest rate on home currency, and

               i_f = the interest rate on foreign currency.

Purchasing Power Parity states that the percentage change in the spot exchange rate of a currency in terms of another will be, on average, equal to the differential of inflation rates between the two countries. Mathematically, it is expressed as follows:

$$E_f = \frac{(1 + I_h)}{(1 + I_f)} - 1$$

where E_f = the change in the spot exchange rate of the foreign currency,

               I_h = the inflation rate in the home country, and

               I_f = the inflation rate in the foreign country.

International Fisher Effect states that the percentage change in the spot exchange rate of a currency in terms of another will, on average, equal to the differential of interest rates between the two countries. Mathematically, it is expressed as follows:

$$E_f = \frac{(1 + i_h)}{(1 + i_f)} - 1$$

where E_f = the change in the spot rate of the foreign currency,

               i_h = the interest rate in the home country, and

               i_f = the interest rate in the foreign country.

22.5 FOREIGN EXCHANGE EXPOSURE

Transaction Exposure takes place when the future cash transactions of a multinational corporation are affected by exchange rate fluctuations. Transaction exposure may be hedged by:

— Investing strategy: if the MNC has future payables denominated in foreign currency, the company should invest in a time deposit denominated in the same currency and maturing at the same time payables become due.

— Borrowing strategy: if the MNC has future receivables denominated in foreign currency, the company should borrow a loan denominated in foreign currency that becomes due at the same time the receivables should be collected.

— Invoicing strategy: MNC may price (invoice) its exports in the same currency that will be needed to pay for its imports.

— Futures contract strategy: exporters may hedge by selling a future contract on the foreign currency, and importers may buy a future contract on the foreign currency.

— Money market hedge: it is similar to the investing strategy mentioned above. The difference is that investing strategy is only used when the MNC has excess cash to invest.

— Currency options strategy: MNC would buy a call option to hedge its future payables denominated in foreign currency and sell call option to hedge its future receivables denominated in foreign currency.

Translation Exposure is the foreign exchange risk which emanates from the accounting need to translate the MNC's consolidated financial statements into the parent home currency.

Economic Exposure can be measured by calculating the difference between the present value of the MNC's future cash flows based on the expected exchange rate, and the present value of the cash flows based on the unexpected exchange rate.

CHAPTER 23

FINANCING SMALL FIRMS AND STARTUPS

23.1 SOURCES OF FINANCING FOR TRADITIONAL SMALL FIRMS

Traditional small firms are small because the nature of the industry enables them to compete with larger firms. Typically, the firms in this category have a localized market, relatively low capital requirements and relatively simple technology. Growth potential is usually not great and expected profitability will not be attractive to outside investors.

Startups require the owners to commit their savings. A mortgage on their home or loans from friends and relatives may be a source of financing. Trade credit usually is an important source; however, this depends upon several factors. A new small business may have to purchase all inventory on C.O.D. terms. If the firm has a unique product, a purchaser may be willing to make advance payments.

Smaller cash infusions, especially for start-ups, can be had by borrowing on life insurance policies or home equity loans, borrowing against CDs and other equities, making a 60-day free roll-over on a traditional IRA, and even credit card loans.

Several government agencies provide direct loans (rare) and guaranteed loans. The most important source is the Small Business Administration (SBA); however, other federal agencies with programs are Farmers Home Administration and the Economic Development Administration. Several states have business loan programs.

Rapid Growth Stage — Trade credit continues as an important source during this period and bank loans are an essential source of financing. Owners need to reinvest as much of their earnings as possible. Bank term loans may be possible, depending upon the demonstrated profitability of the firm. Leasing and installment buying of fixed assets are additional sources. If the potential market looks sufficiently large, a public stock offering may be possible.

Commerical finance companies should not be overlooked. Large finance companies finance accounts receivable, inventory, and fixed assets (asset lending). Finance companies can lend to riskier firms than can banks.

Working capital management and current liability management are especially critical during this stage.

Maturity Stage — The most common types of financing needed by firms in this stage are seasonal loans and term loans for equipment purchases. If the firm has a successful operating record, this stage should be the easiest to finance. The sources are the same as during the rapid growth stage.

Decline — This stage should generate funds through liquidation of assets. External funds may be needed if diversification or new products are involved. A merger may be necessary. Borrowing from traditional sources, except asset-based borrowing, may be difficult. Additional equity may be required.

23.2 SOURCES OF FINANCING FOR FIRMS WITH GROWTH POTENTIAL

The firm with growth potential may use all the sources available to the traditional small firm; however, additional sources may be available to these firms. These additional sources are venture capital firms and public offerings.

Venture Capital is **risk** capital. Venture capital firms typically specialize by industry and by stage of product development. Some venture firms provide seed capital for new product development and startup, others participate in first- or later-stage financing, some provide bridge financing to prepare companies for a public offering and others provide funds for acquisition and buyout.

Venture capital is expensive. A venture firm may expect a 50 percent or more annual return for seed capital and 30 – 40 percent annual return for investments at later stages.

Venture capital is equity capital or debt and equity capital. Venture capitalists actively participate in the firm through the board of directors and typically think of a six- or seven-year involvement, A public offering is the normal way for them to receive their return on investment.

Sources of venture capital funds are private venture capital partnerships, public venture capital funds, industrial venture capital, investment banking firms' venture capital funds, Small Business Investment Companies (SBIC), Minority Enterprise Small Business Investment Companies (MESBIC), individual investors and some state governments.

In the case of a **public offering**, underwriters and investors typically look for a firm with several years of strong, steady growth and increasing profits. Where considerable capital is required, some startups use a public offering.

Firms who have used venture capital financing will typically have grown to the size that a traditional public offering will be required.

Several simplified filing requirements have been developed for small firms who decide to go public. A public offering, however, is expensive for a small firm as accounting fees and attorney fees for preparation of the filing will be costly. Because of the relatively small size of the offering and the risk involved, underwriting fees will also be significant.

The small publicly-held firm has other costs not incurred by the privately-held firm. Records of the Board of Directors, audited financial reports to the stockholders, and public reporting requirements are costs that must be considered by firms prior to the decision to go public.

REA's Test Preps
The Best in Test Preparation

- REA "Test Preps" are **far more** comprehensive than any other test preparation series
- Each book contains up to **eight** full-length practice tests based on the most recent exams
- **Every** type of question likely to be given on the exams is included
- Answers are accompanied by **full** and **detailed** explanations

REA publishes over 60 Test Preparation volumes in several series. They include:

Advanced Placement Exams(APs)
Biology
Calculus AB & Calculus BC
Chemistry
Computer Science
Economics
English Language & Composition
English Literature & Composition
European History
Government & Politics
Physics B & C
Psychology
Spanish Language
Statistics
United States History

College-Level Examination Program (CLEP)
Analyzing and Interpreting Literature
College Algebra
Freshman College Composition
General Examinations
General Examinations Review
History of the United States I
History of the United States II
Human Growth and Development
Introductory Sociology
Principles of Marketing
Spanish

SAT II: Subject Tests
Biology E/M
Chemistry
English Language Proficiency Test
French
German

SAT II: Subject Tests (cont'd)
Literature
Mathematics Level IC, IIC
Physics
Spanish
United States History
Writing

Graduate Record Exams (GREs)
Biology
Chemistry
Computer Science
General
Literature in English
Mathematics
Physics
Psychology

ACT - ACT Assessment

ASVAB - Armed Services Vocational Aptitude Battery

CBEST - California Basic Educational Skills Test

CDL - Commercial Driver License Exam

CLAST - College Level Academic Skills Test

COOP & HSPT - Catholic High School Admission Tests

ELM - California State University Entry Level Mathematics Exam

FE (EIT) - Fundamentals of Engineering Exams - For both AM & PM Exams

FTCE - Florida Teacher Certification Exam

GED - High School Equivalency Diploma Exam (U.S. & Canadian editions)

GMAT CAT - Graduate Management Admission Test

LSAT - Law School Admission Test

MAT- Miller Analogies Test

MCAT - Medical College Admission Test

MTEL - Massachusetts Tests for Educator Licensure

MSAT- Multiple Subjects Assessment for Teachers

NJ HSPA - New Jersey High School Proficiency Assessment

NYSTCE: LAST & ATS-W - New York State Teacher Certification

PLT - Principles of Learning & Teaching Tests

PPST- Pre-Professional Skills Tests

PSAT - Preliminary Scholastic Assessment Test

SAT

TExES - Texas Examinations of Educator Standards

THEA - Texas Higher Education Assessment

TOEFL - Test of English as a Foreign Language

TOEIC - Test of English for International Communication

USMLE Steps 1,2,3 - U.S. Medical Licensing Exams

U.S. Postal Exams 460 & 470

RESEARCH & EDUCATION ASSOCIATION
61 Ethel Road W. • Piscataway, New Jersey 08854
Phone: (732) 819-8880   **website: www.rea.com**

Please send me more information about your Test Prep books

Name _____

Address _____

City _____ State _____ Zip _____